such Offences, such as Forfeiture of Life, Confifcation of Lands, &c. &c. And I do hereby farther declare all indented Servants, Negroes, or others (appertaining to Rebels) free, that are able and willing to bear Arms, they joining his Majefty's Troops, as foon as may be, for the more fpeedily reducing this Colony to a proper Senfe of their Duty, to his Majefty's Crown and Dignity. I do farther order, and require, all his Majefty's liege Subjects to retain their Quitrents, or any other Taxes due, or that may become due, in their own Cuftody, till fuch Time as Peace may be again reftored to this at prefent moft unhappy Country, or demanded of them for their former falutary Purpofes, by Officers properly authorifed to receive the fame.

GIVEN under my Hand, on Board the Ship William, off Norfolk, the 7th Day of November, in the 16th Year of his Majefty's Reign.

DUNMORE.

GOD SAVE THE KING.

A Copy

1776.

America.

have connected them with another, and to
require that they

2,00 2,05 3,00 3,10 3,15

Fl. Moose

Mistassin See

CANADA

Adirondaks oder Algonkins

PROVINZ QUEBEK

NEU SCHOTTLAND ACADIEN

S. Laurens Flu

Golfo von St. Laurenz

Huron See

Ontario See

Michigan See

NH

M

NY

C

R

PNS

MRL

DW

VIRGINIEN

NORTH CAROLINA

SOUTH CAROLINA

GEORGIA

FLORIDA

ATLANTISCHES MEER

In Staten Island.
1. Richmond.
In Neu Iersey.
2. Newark.
3. Elisabethtown.
4. Morrestown.
In Pensylvanien.
5. Germantown.
6. Bristol.
7. Chester.
8. Middleton.
9. Ephrata.
10. Manheim.
11. Hummelstown.

CHARTE
über die XIII. vereinigte
Staaten von
NORD-AMERICA
Entworfen durch F. L. Güssefeld
und herausgegeben von den
Homännischen Erben.
Mit Römisch Kayserl. Allergn.
Freyheit A.° 1784.

Erlæuterung der grossen Buchstaben.

M. Provinz Massachusets Bay. NH. New Hampshire.
R. Rhode-Island. C. Connecticut. NY. New York.
NJ. New Jersey. PNS. Pensylvanien. DW. Delaware.
MRL. Maryland. Die übrigen vier Provinzen sind auf der Char...

Geographische Meilen 15. auf 1. Grad.

See-Meilen 20. auf einen Grad.

Englændis. Meilen 69 ½ auf einen Grad.

Image credits: Ride of Paul Revere: Hy Hintermeister (public domain); horse engraving: Channarong Pherngjanda/Shutterstock.com; page border: Dn Br/Shutterstock.com; free Black woman in New Orleans (public domain); Dunmore Proclamation (Library of Congress/rbpe17801800); Benjamin Franklin portrait: Joseph-Siffred Duplessis (National Portrait Gallery/public domain); spoon engraving: Marzufello/Shutterstock.com; bridge engraving, fort engraving, Charleson engraving, hilltop engraving, rifle engraving, wagon wheel engraving, swamp engraving, soldier engraving, drum engraving: Morphart Creation/Shutterstock.com; teacup engraving: JimmyIurii/Shutterstock.com; quill engraving, cannonball engraving: sharpner/Shutterstock.com; hands holding paper engraving: Maisei Raman/Shutterstock.com; grave engraving: GoodStudio/Shutterstock.com; Revolutionary War medals: The Society of the Cincinnati, Washington, D.C. (used with permission); Mercy Otis Warren: John Singleton Copley (Museum of Fine Arts/public domain); Washington Crossing the Delaware: Emanuel Leutze (The Metropolitan Museum of Art/public domain); Phillis Wheatley book: Houghton Library (public domain); Nancy Hart illustration: Stories of Georgia by Joel Chandler Harris (public domain); Francis Marion illustration: John Blake White (Library of Congress/2014646166); The Death of General Warren at the Battle of Bunker Hill: John Trumbull (Boston Museum of Fine Arts/public domain); Joseph Brant: Charles Willson Peale (Independence National Historical Park/public domain); watercolor of uniforms: Jean-Baptiste-Antoine DeVerger (Brown University Library/public domain); James Armistead affidavit: Virginia Historical Society (public domain); Royal Proclamation of 1763 map (public domain); painting of pitcher: Jean Baptiste Siméon Chardin (public domain); Native American pattern: Moon Meadows/Shutterstock.com; Native American border: Dimas Adi/Shutterstock.com; envelope engraving, book engraving: MoreVector/Shutterstock.com; plaque engraving: Alexander_P/Shutterstock.com; quill and ink engraving: MoreVector/Shutterstock.com; farm painting: John Lewin (Mitchell Library/public domain); Siege of Yorktown painting: Auguste Couder (Galerie des Batailles/public domain); Grand Union flag (public domain); Betsy Ross flag (public domain); sewing needle engraving: Istry Istry/Shutterstock.com; Lafayette portrait: Charles Willson Peale (Independence National Historical Park/public domain); Baron von Steuben portrait: Ralph Earl (Yale University Art Gallery/public domain); laundry engraving: Bodor Tivadar/Shutterstock.com; Admiral de Grasse portrait: Jean-Baptiste Mauzaisse (Joconde/public domain); Rochambeau: Jean-Baptiste Mauzaisse (Joconde/public domain); Schweikart portrait: Karl Gottlieb Schweikart (National Museum in Warsaw/public domain); Mazzei portrait: Jacques-Louis David (Joconde/public domain); Townshend portrait: Gilbert Stuart (State Library of New South Wales/public domain); Boswell portrait: Joshua Reynolds (National Portrait Gallery/public domain); Pitt portrait: George Romney (Tate/public domain); redcoats: Howard Pyle (Scribner's Magazine/public domain); bluecoats: Henry Ogden (Library of Congress/92515475); French uniforms, tricorne hat: John Lossing (Library of Congress/99400771); Hessian uniform (public domain); greencoats: Joshua Reynolds (National Gallery/public domain); cockade (public domain); Battle of Rhode Island map (Library of Congress/00555648); Deborah Sampson portrait: George Graham (Massachusetts Historical Society/public domain); Ann Bates (History of American Women/public domain); John Adams portrait: Benjamin Blyth (Massachusetts Historical Society/public domain); invisible ink (New York Public Library/public domain); Boston Massacre: Paul Revere (Metropolitan Museum of Art/public domain); Jenner: Ernest Board (public domain); mortar and pestle engraving: Channarong Pherngjanda/Shutterstock.com; Macaroni: Philip Dawe (Lewis Walpole Library/public domain); The Old Plantation: John Rose (Abby Aldrich Rockefeller Folk Art Museum/public domain); A Society of Patriotic Ladies at Edenton in North Carolina (British Museum/public domain): Sir Walter Raleigh portrait: William Segar (National Gallery of Ireland/public domain); French and Indian War: Hervey Smyth (Library of the Canadian Department of National Defence/public domain); Patrick Henry: Peter F. Rothermel (public domain); Boston Tea Party (public domain); Declaration of Independence: John Trumbull (public domain); Battle of Lexington and Concord: William Barnes Wollen (National Army Museum/public domain); Surrender at Yorktown: John Trumbull (public domain); Independence Hall (Library of Congress/ 2003665196); privateer: Ambroise Louis Garneray (Musée d'Histoire de Saint-Malo/public domain); Puritans: George Henry Boughton (New York Historical Society/public domain); courtroom: George Cooke (Virginia Historical Society/public domain); Native American slavery: Benjamin West (Library of Congress/2012647230); Lord Dunmore portrait: Joshua Reynolds (Scottish National Gallery/public domain); Peter Salem portrait: Walter J. Williams, Jr. (Revolutionary War Journal/public domain); General George Washington portrait: Charles Willson Peale (Brooklyn Museum/public domain); state flags (public domain); Sierra Leone: John Leighton Wilson (Western Africa: Its History, Condition, and Prospects/public domain); Scene at the Signing of the Constitution of the United States: Howard Chandler Christy (public domain); A Liverpool Slave Ship: William Jackson (Merseyside Maritime Museum/public domain); US Capitol: William Birch (Library of Congress/2004661947); Storming Fort Wagner: Kurz & Allison (Library of Congress/2012647346); slave trade print: Everett Collection/Shutterstock.com; all patterns licensed from various Shutterstock.com artists; paper texture: Lukasz Szwaj/Shutterstock.com; Thirteen Colonies map (public domain); Betsy Ross flag: David Smart/Shutterstock.com; French cockade: Claudio Divizia/Shutterstock.com.

LCCN: 2022931178
ISBN: 9781638190929

First Edition

Printed in China

10 9 8 7 6 5 4 3 2

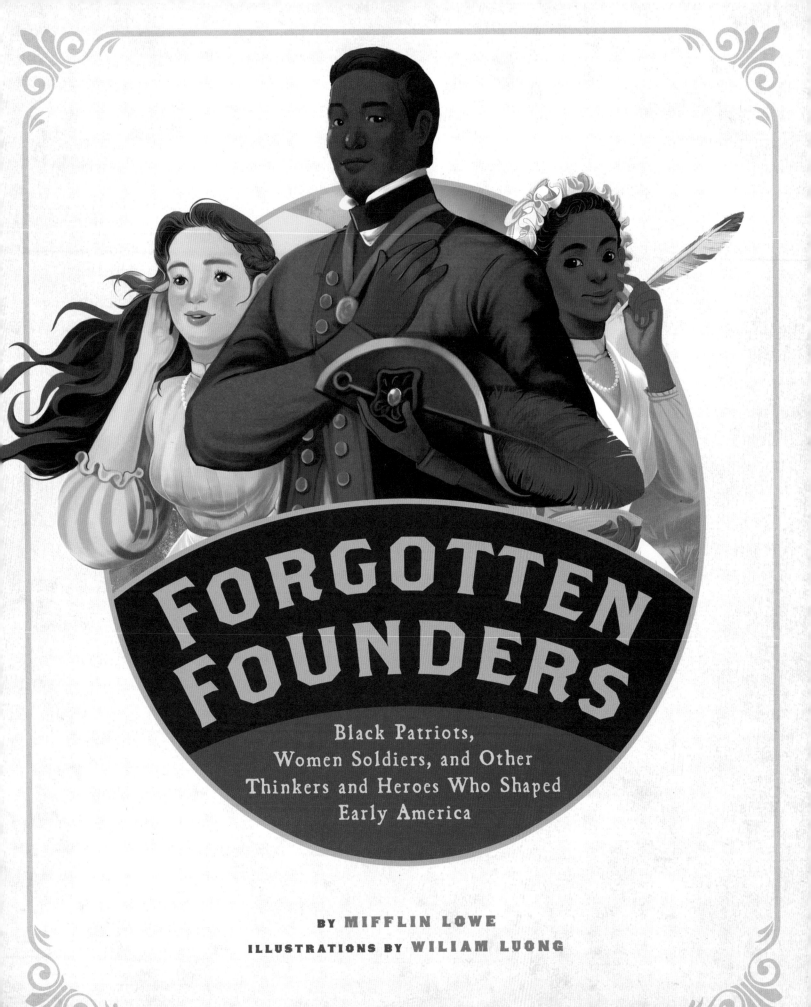

FORGOTTEN FOUNDERS

Black Patriots, Women Soldiers, and Other Thinkers and Heroes Who Shaped Early America

BY **MIFFLIN LOWE**

ILLUSTRATIONS BY **WILIAM LUONG**

CONTENTS

AUTHOR'S NOTE

Whoa, Did I Have a Lot to Learn!

f course, I knew a fair amount about George Washington, John Adams, Thomas Jefferson, Benjamin Franklin, and the other people known as our Founding Fathers. They are justifiably famous. As they said in the last sentence of the Declaration of Independence, "We mutually pledge to each other our lives, our fortunes, and our sacred honor"—and they meant it. Never in history did so many people of such brilliance and conviction pursue a path that would change the world forever.

But they did not—indeed, could not have achieved—what they did without the Forgotten Founders introduced in these pages. I confess, before researching this book, I knew almost nothing about the women and people of color who were also a part of the American Revolution. Make no mistake: these were not historical footnotes. These men and women were brave, passionate Patriots without whom the country could never have succeeded in the struggle to replace the rule of kings and queens with democratic institutions and, ultimately, give us all the right to "life, liberty, and the pursuit of happiness."

Yes, there were lots of contradictions when this country was started. The Constitution and Bill of Rights were remarkable documents when it came to stating the principles of freedom and enunciating the ideal of liberty for all. And yet, at the time they were written, nearly all thirteen colonies allowed enslavement and gave few legal rights to women.

Those contradictions—the gaps between the ideal and the reality—are what make these stories all the more compelling to me. In practice, the people you meet in this book had, in some ways, less to gain in the fight for independence than property-owning white colonists, and yet they fought as fiercely and willingly as any. Slaves joined up in hopes of emancipation—a promise that was not universally kept. Women went to arms and endured tremendous sacrifice in the name of free government—though they couldn't participate in that government for more than another hundred years. It was a complex affair, yet it was carried out by people who believed in principles we're still working to live up to today. Some of these people you'll already know. Most you won't. All of them can inspire us to continue the hard, worthy work of trying to actually live those most famous of words: "We hold these truths to be self-evident, that all men are created equal."

In the end, the point of this book is not to rewrite history or dismiss the people long known as our Founding Fathers—or make the lives of women, Native Americans, or Blacks sound better than they were. Instead, the goal is to broaden our perspective and celebrate those who generally have yet to be sufficiently recognized—to make the story of the founding of this country everyone's story, for everyone's it is.

—Mifflin Lowe

INTRODUCTION

To fully appreciate the people and events in this book, it's helpful to have some background about what the Revolutionary War was, why it happened, and what life was like for people who lived during that time.

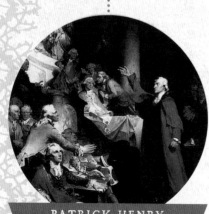

HOW THE REVOLUTIONARY WAR CAME TO BE

Things begin way back in 1585, when Sir Walter Raleigh founded the first British colony on the island of Roanoke, now part of North Carolina. The settlers at Roanoke mysteriously disappeared (that's another tale), and a new colony was established in Jamestown, Virginia. Over the next 150 years, thirteen British colonies would appear on American soil, from New Hampshire in the north to Georgia in the south.

At first, these colonies had a great deal of freedom to govern themselves. After all, Great Britain was miles away, across the Atlantic Ocean. Many colonies had governing bodies of elected representatives, like the Virginia House of Burgesses, that passed their own laws.

The French and Indian War

Great Britain wasn't the only country with colonies in America. France, Spain, and other European countries wanted land and influence in America, and war eventually broke out. The French and Indian War lasted from 1754 until 1763, when the Treaty of Paris was signed. Though Great Britain won the war and most of the land east of the Mississippi River, that victory came with a cost: debt, and *lots* of it.

The British government needed a way to pay for all the bills that were stacking up. They came up with what seemed like a brilliant idea: tax the colonies! After all, weren't the colonists the ones who benefited most from the victory?

Taxation without Representation

When new taxes poured in on everything from tea to paper to glass to playing cards, they were furious. They protested the taxes and demanded

As you prepare to read the stories in the next part of the book, think about what America was like at the time. What freedom were people fighting for? Could there be more than one?

BOSTON TEA PARTY

representation in Parliament. Sometimes things got violent, like when American colonists tarred and feathered British tax collectors or destroyed 342 chests of tea in the Boston Tea Party. Now it was Britain's turn to be furious. Parliament responded with laws designed to punish the colonies, like closing the Boston port and dissolving some colonial legislatures.

The First Continental Congress

The time for action had come. In 1774, twelve of the thirteen colonies sent delegates to meet in Philadelphia and discuss what should be done. First, they decided to stop importing British goods. Then, they wrote a declaration of rights to send to Parliament.

CONGRESS DECLARES
INDEPENDENCE

The Second Continental Congress

In May of 1775, the congress met again. Parliament had ignored the declaration of rights, British troops had clashed with colonial militias at Lexington and Concord, and war was upon them. George Washington was appointed to lead the American army. But even then, some hoped for reconciliation with Great Britain. The colonists sent a letter to King George III, the British king, declaring their loyalty and seeking a path to peace.

Independence Declared

Peace was not to be. Instead, King George declared that the colonists were in open rebellion and sent more British troops and even German mercenaries to fight the colonies. Support for independence among the colonists had gone from simmering to boiling, and in the summer of 1776, the congress officially declared independence from Great Britain. The war that had started with a skirmish in Lexington and Concord grew into a seven-year engagement that cost over 50,000 American, British, German, and French lives. Finally, in 1781, British General Lord Cornwallis surrendered to Washington at Yorktown, Virginia, and in 1783, the Treaty of Paris led to the end of the war. America was a free and independent nation.

THE BATTLE OF
LEXINGTON & CONCORD

BRITISH SURRENDER
AT YORKTOWN

PEOPLE OF COLONIAL TIMES

When you hear things like "Revolutionary War" or "Declaration of Independence," the first thing that pops in your head might be a man wearing a white wig. And for good reason! Most paintings (like all the ones on the previous two pages) and stories about the Revolution are about people like George Washington, Thomas Jefferson, and Benjamin Franklin—names and faces that are still well-known today.

What is not as well understood is that between 2 and 2.5 million people lived in America at the time, and they had as profound an impact on the Revolution as the men sitting in Congress—though their lives looked very different.

Women in Colonial America

Generally speaking, women in colonial America were expected to run a household and perform domestic duties, such as spinning, sewing, preserving food, taking care of farm animals, cooking, cleaning, and raising children. Girls were homeschooled or educated at "dame" schools, which taught only basic reading and math. (Frankly, most boys were also barely educated. One-room schoolhouses were often located in the middle of roads because no one wanted to use good farmland for schools.)

WOMEN LATER ON

Over time, things gradually changed. In 1771, New York State passed a law requiring a man to get his wife's signature to sell property. In 1848, The Married Women's Property Act, one of the most important property laws in American history, allowed women to own and control property. On August 18, 1920, the Nineteenth Amendment became part of the US Constitution and gave women the right to vote. Today, though a long way from the days of Abigail Adams, equality continues to be a matter of cultural and political discussion.

FEW RIGHTS FOR WOMEN

Colonial-era women were expected to marry by age twenty and had few rights:

- *Women were not allowed to vote.*
- *Women were not allowed to hold public office.*
- *Married women could not make a will.*
- *Married women could not own property. (Widows and unmarried women had more rights than married women. They were allowed to buy and sell property, make a will, and sign a contract. Widows received one-third of their husband's property when he died.)*

WHERE DID SLAVES COME FROM?

Typically, slaves were purchased by Europeans from African tribes who had captured people from other African tribes and enslaved them. Out of 10.7 million slaves shipped to the Western hemisphere, over 90 percent—about 10.4 million people—were taken to Caribbean and South American countries. About 388,000 people came to the colonies as slaves.

African Americans in Colonial America

From earliest colonial days, slavery was practiced in all thirteen colonies. Even colonies with fewer slaves still benefited from the slave trade and slave labor, creating a complicated economic web.

During the time of the Revolution, slaves faced difficult decisions. Great Britain offered freedom to those who escaped and agreed to fight for the British. Some American masters offered freedom to those who fought for the Patriots, while still others allowed slaves to use their army wages to buy their freedom. Far more slaves joined the British than the Americans.

Despite promises from both sides, things remained complicated for African Americans after the war. Those who fought for the Patriots often had difficulty securing freedom and pay. Those who fought for the British had to flee the country or risk being returned to their masters.

After America's founding, slavery continued to be a contested, complex issue. On one hand, slavery was increasingly considered immoral by a growing number of people. On the other hand, slave labor was becoming a significant part of the era's economic system. The debate between these rising trends would continue until it finally boiled over in the American Civil War, more than seventy years after the country's founding.

1619:
Approximately twenty enslaved people arrive at Point Comfort, Virginia, near Jamestown. They are brought by British privateers (pirates), who seized them from a captured Portuguese slave ship.

1777, JULY 2:
Vermont becomes the first colony to abolish slavery when it ratifies its first constitution and becomes a sovereign country. (There were approximately twenty-five slaves in Vermont at the time.)

1641:
Massachusetts becomes the first colony to recognize slavery as a legal institution.

1777, JANUARY:
The colonies' inability to fill soldier quotas forces Washington to reverse his decision about barring free Blacks from fighting for the Patriots, and he allows them to enlist.

1654:
A Virginia court gives free Blacks the right to hold slaves.

1775:
Lord Dunmore, the British governor of Virginia, offers freedom to slaves who escape Patriot masters and join the Loyalists (colonists who supported the British).

1670-1715:
Native American slaves, often captured in intertribal war, outnumber African slaves brought to the colonies. Between 24,000 and 51,000 are exported from South Carolina alone.

1775:
Days after taking command after the Battle of Bunker Hill, George Washington decrees that no Black, free or enslaved, can be recruited to fight. He does this because slaveholding states fear a rebellion if slaves are allowed to carry weapons.

1735-1750:
Georgia is the only British American colony to prohibit Black slavery as a matter of public policy.

1775:
Free Black soldiers fight for the Patriots in battles at Lexington, Concord, and Bunker Hill.

1778:

Rhode Island promises to free all Black, Indian, and mulatto slaves who enlist in the new 1st Rhode Island Regiment. More than 140 Black men sign up for what becomes known as the "Black Regiment."

In the first two decades after the American Revolution, state legislatures take actions to free slaves.

1780:

Pennsylvania declares that all Black children born slaves will be freed at age twenty-eight.

1781–1783:

In the Quock Walker case, the Supreme Judicial Court of Massachusetts abolishes slavery by declaring it incompatible with the state constitution. Slave owners replace enslavement with indentured servitude or paid employment.

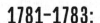

1783:

After the Treaty of Paris, many African Americans who fought for the crown flee with the British Army to the Caribbean, Nova Scotia, England, and Sierra Leone, a new country started by freed slaves in Africa.

1788:

The "Three-Fifths Clause" in the US Constitution increases the political power of slaveholding states who otherwise may not have joined the United States.

Slavery is still a grim reality. In 2016, the Global Slavery Index counted 45.8 million enslaved people in 167 countries, with one in four victims being children.

1865:

Near the end of the Civil War—in which between 620,000 and 750,000 people die—the Thirteenth Amendment to the United States Constitution abolishes slavery in every state and territory of the United States.

1807:

The "Act Prohibiting Importation of Slaves of 1807" is a United States federal law that says no new slaves can be imported into the United States. By this time, all Northern states have passed laws outlawing slavery, either immediately or over time.

1799:

In his will, George Washington frees all the enslaved people he owned.

1794:

The Slave Trade Act ends the legality of American ships participating in the trade.

1790:

When the first census is taken, African Americans number about 760,000, approximately 19 percent of the population. (In 2020, the Black percentage of the US population was 12.4 percent.)

SYBIL LUDINGTON

The Female Paul Revere (Who Did What He Couldn't)

Who rode a horse forty miles to warn American colonists about British soldiers on the march? Not Paul Revere. He rode only about twenty miles—and was captured by British soldiers. It was a sixteen-year-old girl, Sybil Ludington, who completed the courageous night ride.

At 9:00 PM on April 26, 1777, Sybil saddled up her horse, Star, and rode through the darkness and rain over a rough, rocky road to warn the colonists that the British were headed for Danbury, Connecticut, where the Continental Army kept supplies. Along the way, armed with only a stick, Sybil is said to have fought off an outlaw trying to rob her. By the time she got to Danbury, it was too late to save the town (the British had burned it), but Sybil was able to gather 400 militiamen. In the morning, her militiamen forced the British to retreat in the Battle of Ridgefield.

In honor of her bravery, Sybil was personally thanked by George Washington and General Rochambeau, the French commander who fought alongside the Patriots. Alexander Hamilton wrote, "I congratulate you on the Danbury expedition."

Although people soon forgot about Sybil, in 1912, a poem by Fred C. Warner titled *On an April Night 1777*, written like Henry Wadsworth Longfellow's famous 1860 *Midnight Ride of Paul Revere*, renewed the story of her bravery. Then, in the 1930s, the New York State Education Department posted historical-marker signs at her home and along the route of her ride through Putnam County. In 1940, a statue of Sybil and her horse, Star, was erected in Carmel, New York. And in 1975, Ludington became the thirty-fifth woman to be honored on a United States postage stamp.

NIGHT RIDERS

In Massachusetts, three riders—William Dawes, Samuel Prescott, and Paul Revere—were sent to warn Concord that "the British were coming" to capture the guns and gunpowder stored there. Prescott was the only one who made it to Concord; Revere was captured, and Dawes was thrown off his horse and forced to walk home.

THINK DEEPER

Sybil was only sixteen years old when she rode to warn Danbury, but the people listened to her. Does a person have to be old to change history?

ODE TO SYBIL

Fred C. Warner's 1912 poem, On an April Night 1777, mimicked Henry Wadsworth Longfellow's famous Midnight Ride of Paul Revere. Here are the beginning lines.

ON AN APRIL NIGHT 1777

Listen my children and you shall hear
Of the midnight ride of Sybil Ludington,
On the twenty-sixth of April, in Seventy-seven;
Hardly a man is now alive
Who remembers that famous day and year.

JAMES ARMISTEAD LAFAYETTE

BORN: 1748, NEW KENT COUNTY, VIRGINIA | DIED: 1830, BALTIMORE, MARYLAND

The Secret Agent Who Helped Win the War

Born into slavery in 1748, James Armistead lived on a plantation in Virginia. During the American Revolution, James received permission from his master, William Armistead, to enlist in the Marquis de Lafayette's French allied units.

But James didn't just enlist as a regular soldier. He became a spy. Telling the British he was a runaway slave who wanted to serve the Loyalist cause, James was, in fact, a double agent who pretended to work for the British but *really* worked for the Americans. This let him learn important details about British plans and hand over important information to his American commander—while giving the British false information about the Patriots.

In 1781, during a critical moment in the Revolution, James told Lafayette and Washington about British General Lord Cornwallis's move to Yorktown, Virginia, and the expected arrival of 10,000 British troops. His information led to a resounding American victory, and the British were forced to surrender on October 17, 1781—effectively ending the Revolutionary War.

Although Americans celebrated freedom throughout the United States at the end of the war, James, despite his contributions to victory, could not. Because he was a spy and not a soldier, he was not covered by the Act of 1783, which freed any enslaved soldiers who fought for the Revolution. James was forced, once again, to be a slave.

Immediately, James asked Congress for his freedom. After years without success, Armistead finally received assistance from the Marquis de Lafayette, who wrote a letter

VICTORY AT YORKTOWN

Once the Americans knew Cornwallis had moved to Yorktown (thanks to James), they carried out a plan with the French fleet, under Admiral de Grasse, and the combined French and American armies (pictured above) to surround the enemy with a blockade at sea and a siege* on land. Combined with constant bombardment, this resulted in a decisive victory.

THINK DEEPER

Even though he served valiantly, why do you think James had such a hard time winning his freedom?

(see image on right) to Congress that told of James's courage and intelligence. That did the trick, and in 1787, Armistead was awarded his freedom. Adding "Lafayette" to his name in honor of the French general, James lived the rest of his life as a free man. In 1824, he and Lafayette met again during Lafayette's grand tour of the United States, where the general picked James out of a crowd and gave him a hug.

With an annual army pension, Armistead eventually moved to his own forty-acre farm in Virginia, where he married, raised a family, and became a wealthy farmer.

*"SIEGE" MEANS SURROUNDING A FORTIFIED PLACE SO THAT PEOPLE AND SUPPLIES CAN'T GET THROUGH TO IT.

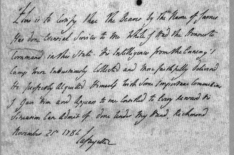

NANCY HART

A Patriot with the "Heart" of a Lion

ne unforgettable character from the South* was Nancy Ann Morgan Hart. Called "Aunt Nancy," she was a tall (six feet), muscular, rawboned woman with red hair and a face scarred by smallpox. Even though she was cross-eyed, she was an excellent shot. And with her hotheaded temper and fearless spirit, she was a woman you didn't want to mess with.

Once, six Loyalist** soldiers stopped at her cabin looking for a Patriot they were chasing. When they demanded that Hart cook her only turkey for them, she cunningly agreed. Before sitting down to eat, the Loyalists put their guns near the door. When they weren't paying attention, Nancy grabbed a rifle and ordered them to stay still. When one moved, she shot and killed him. When another made a move toward the weapons, she shot him, too, and held the rest at gunpoint until her husband and neighbors showed up. Supposedly, her husband wanted to shoot the soldiers, but Nancy insisted they be hanged. And they were.

On other occasions, dressed as a man and pretending to be feeble-minded, Nancy went to British camps, spied on their doings, and passed the information on to the Patriots. Nancy would have been hanged if she'd been caught—talk about gumption!

Over the years, Georgia has honored Nancy Hart with named places like Hart County; its county seat, Hartwell; Lake Hartwell; Hartwell Dam; and Nancy Hart Highway (Georgia Route 77). The Georgia chapter of the National Society of the Daughters of the American Revolution was even renamed in her honor.

*SPEAKING OF "FORGOTTEN FOUNDERS," IT SOMETIMES SEEMS THE SOUTHERN COLONIES ARE A BIT NEGLECTED IN HISTORIES OF THE REVOLUTIONARY WAR. IN FACT, THE FIGHTING THERE WAS EVERY BIT AS FIERCE AND IMPORTANT AS THE WARFARE IN THE NORTH—AND THE PEOPLE EVERY BIT AS COMMITTED AND BRAVE.

**LOYALISTS WERE COLONISTS WHO SUPPORTED THE BRITISH.

SWAMP FOX

Francis Marion, nicknamed "The Swamp Fox," was a leader of the Continental Army in South Carolina. A master of guerilla war tactics, he used surprise attacks and sudden withdrawals to harass and confuse the British. He was hated and pursued by the British, who said, "the Devil himself could not catch this old fox."

When the Loyalist soldiers put their guns by the door, they clearly didn't expect Nancy to use them. Why?

WEAPON OF CHOICE

Handy for hunting as well as for war, the American long rifle was the most accurate weapon in the colonial era. Used by snipers and infantry, the grooved barrels had a range of 300 yards (compared to 100 yards for smoothbore muskets).

MYSTERY SOLVED

Did the story of Nancy and the Loyalist soldiers really happen? In 1912, construction crews working on the railroad near the site of Nancy's cabin found six old skeletons buried in a row. A few had broken necks, showing they had, indeed, been hanged until dead.

CUFFEE WELLS SAUNDERS

Talented Medical Man

Cuffee Wells Saunders was born in Guiana, South America. As a child, he was sent to Connecticut to live as a slave for a doctor in Hartford. Later, he became an apothecary (pharmacist) for Deacon Israel Wells of Colchester, Connecticut.

In order to gain his freedom, Cuffee enlisted in the Continental Army in 1777 as a private in the 4th Connecticut Regiment.* Saunders's considerable medical skill, which he'd learned from his first master, was quickly noticed by his military superiors and put to use. He was assigned duty as a "waiter," or assistant, to Dr. Philip Turner, the surgeon general of the hospital of the Northern Division of the Army, to help prepare medicines and perform medical procedures. Thanks to his abilities, he was soon called "Doctor Cuffee."

In 1778, Cuffee was transferred from Connecticut to Valley Forge, Pennsylvania, where he worked as a medical assistant from June to September. Afterward, he returned to the 4th Connecticut in Danbury, Connecticut, and spent the rest of the war there. Following the war, Cuffee gained his emancipation by giving the money he got for enlisting to his former master as payment for his freedom. After the war, he continued to work with Dr. Turner as an attendant in a local hospital, gaining prestige and recognition throughout his community.

Years later, Cuffee's son, Prince Saunders, attended Dartmouth College and helped set up a Black school system in both Massachusetts and Haiti. Sadly, Cuffee himself died all too soon in December 1788 from influenza.

*THE ALL-BLACK SECOND COMPANY OF THE FOURTH CONNECTICUT REGIMENT, WITH FORTY-EIGHT BLACK PRIVATES AND NONCOMMISSIONED OFFICERS, WAS FORMED IN OCTOBER 1780 AND SERVED UNTIL NOVEMBER 1782.

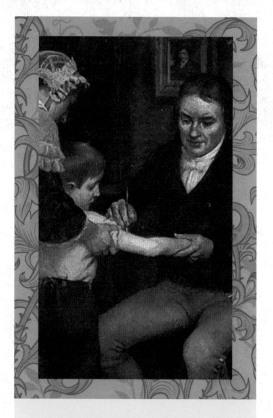

INOCULATION

After several smallpox outbreaks among his troops, General Washington decided to inoculate the entire army in 1777. To do this, a string contaminated with the illness was run through an open cut on a healthy person, who then developed a milder case of the disease (and eventually immunity). Whether Cuffee helped with these inoculations is unknown.

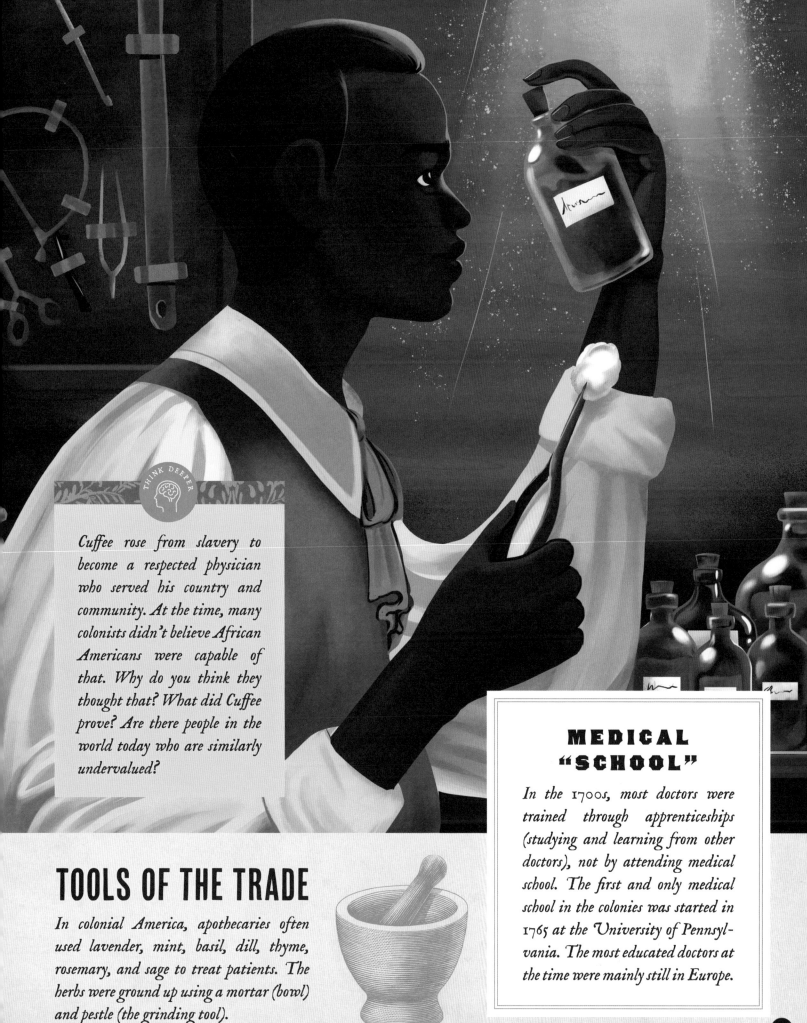

THINK DEEPER

Cuffee rose from slavery to become a respected physician who served his country and community. At the time, many colonists didn't believe African Americans were capable of that. Why do you think they thought that? What did Cuffee prove? Are there people in the world today who are similarly undervalued?

TOOLS OF THE TRADE

In colonial America, apothecaries often used lavender, mint, basil, dill, thyme, rosemary, and sage to treat patients. The herbs were ground up using a mortar (bowl) and pestle (the grinding tool).

MEDICAL "SCHOOL"

In the 1700s, most doctors were trained through apprenticeships (studying and learning from other doctors), not by attending medical school. The first and only medical school in the colonies was started in 1765 at the University of Pennsylvania. The most educated doctors at the time were mainly still in Europe.

SALEM POOR

BORN: 1747, SALEM, MASSACHUSETTS | DIED: 1802, BOSTON, MASSACHUSETTS

Born a Slave, Became a Hero

Salem Poor was born a slave on a farm near Salem, Massachusetts. By 1769, he'd purchased his freedom, and in 1775, he joined the fight for independence as one of the African Americans* who fought at the Battle of Bunker Hill.** Even though the British army was twice as large as the American force, the Americans pushed back their first two assaults. Finally, during the third assault, the Patriots ran out of ammunition and had to retreat. During that battle, Salem was given credit for firing the shot that hit British Lieutenant Colonel James Abercrombie, who later died.***

Six months after Bunker Hill, fourteen officers, including Colonel William Prescott, called Salem a hero and asked the General Court of Massachusetts to honor him. They wrote, "We declare that a Negro man called Salem Poor of Col. Frye's Regiment . . . behaved like an experienced officer as well as an excellent soldier. To set forth particulars of his conduct would be tedious; we would only beg leave to say in the person of this Negro centers a brave and gallant soldier."

In 1776, Salem enlisted in the Continental Army for a three-year term. First, he served at Saratoga, New York (the Patriots won). Next, he spent the winter at Valley Forge, Pennsylvania (the Patriots froze). Finally, he fought in the Battle of White Plains, New York (the Patriots lost). Two hundred years later, in 1976, Salem was honored with a stamp during the celebration of the United States Bicentennial.

THE FATE OF THE COLONEL

During the Battle of Bunker Hill, British Colonel James Abercrombie led a battalion of grenadiers. These were often some of the toughest soldiers in the army, and they sometimes threw grenades. As pictured above, Colonel Abercrombie—the one on the ground—was wounded in the thigh by Salem (or perhaps by friendly fire). He was treated for his injuries but died a week later from the wounds.

*MAYBE THERE WERE THIRTY-SIX AFRICAN AMERICANS THERE. MAYBE 150. NO ONE KNOWS FOR SURE.

**IT'S CALLED THE BATTLE OF BUNKER HILL, EVEN THOUGH IT WAS FOUGHT ON BREED'S HILL, REMEMBER?

***ABERCROMBIE MAY HAVE BEEN HIT BY A BRITISH BULLET. IN WAR, THERE'S A LOT THAT'S UNCERTAIN.

THINK DEEPER

After purchasing his freedom, Salem decided to fight for the Patriots. Why do you think he did this, when most African Americans sided with the British? What would you have done in his position?

A COMPELLING OFFER

Historians estimate than some 5,000 free and enslaved African Americans fought for the Patriots, while approximately 20,000 sided with the British, who promised freedom in return for military service. For example, see the proclamation to the left that was issued by the royal governor of Virginia.

By his Excellency the Right Honourable JOHN Earl of DUNMORE, his Majesty's Lieutenant and Governour-General of the Colony and Dominion of Virginia, and Vice-Admiral of the same:

A PROCLAMATION.

AS I have ever entertained Hopes that an Accommodation might have taken Place between Great Britain and this Colony, without being compelled, by my Duty, to this most disagreeable, but now absolutely necessary Step, rendered so by a Body of armed Men, unlawfully assembled, firing on his Majesty's Tenders, and the Formation of an Army, and that Army now on their March to attack his Majesty's Troops, and destroy the well-disposed Subjects of this Colony: To defeat such treasonable Purposes, and that all such Traitors, and their Abettors, may be brought to Justice, and that the Peace and good Order of this Colony may be again restored, which the ordinary Course of the civil Law is unable to effect, I have thought fit to issue this my Proclamation, hereby declaring, that until the aforesaid good Purposes can be obtained, I do, in Virtue of the Power and Authority to me given, by his Majesty, determine to execute martial Law, and cause the same to be executed throughout this Colony; and to the d that Peace and good Order may the sooner be restored, I do require

WHICH SIDE WOULD YOU FIGHT FOR?

ANNA SMITH STRONG

BORN: 1740, EAST SETAUKET, NEW YORK | DIED: 1812, EAST SETAUKET, NEW YORK

The Clothesline Spy

Anna Smith Strong *was* strong. She was also smart, stealthy, and sly. You see, Anna was a critical part of the spy group known as the Culper Spy Ring, which gave George Washington information on what the British were doing in and around New York City.

It worked like this. First, the spy ring got information from spies in New York City (see Foreign Aid: Hercules Mulligan, on page 46), which they would give to Anna's neighbor on Long Island, Abraham Woodhull. It was then Anna's job to signal another spy, Caleb Brewster, who commanded whale boats on Long Island Sound, that information was ready to pick up.

Anna came up with a brilliant way to do this. She hung her laundry on her clothesline—in plain sight of British soldiers—along with a number of handkerchiefs. Her black petticoat was the signal that a message was ready. The number of handkerchiefs let Caleb know where the message could be found in one of the six coves on Long Island's coast.

Throughout the war, this messaging system worked perfectly. Without ever being discovered, it provided critical intelligence, including plans for a surprise attack on the French forces in Newport, Rhode Island, and a British plan to ruin the American economy by printing counterfeit Continental dollars. The Culper Ring even uncovered Benedict Arnold, the traitor who was plotting to give the American fort at West Point to the British.

As a woman, Anna Strong was severely underestimated by the British, and she shrewdly used this to help her country. By simply doing her laundry, she saved lives and helped win the war. Thanks to her brains and guts, neither Anna nor anyone else in the Culper Ring was ever caught throughout the entire Revolution!

INVISIBLE INK

The Culper Ring sometimes used invisible ink in their secret messages. This was made from a mixture of ferrous sulfate and water and could be revealed by heating the invisible message over the flame of a candle. Benedict Arnold, the Patriot-turned-traitor, also used invisible ink to hide messages in his letters (see real example above).

Washington relied on courageous, everyday colonists like Anna to help win the war. What can a person do today to help change the world and make it a better place?

PETTICOATS

Anna used a black petticoat to signal a message was ready. A petticoat was a garment worn under a dress. For extra warmth, colonial women would sometimes wear more than one.

AGENT 355

During the war, there was a mysterious female agent known only as Agent 355. Many people think this was Anna, but nobody knows for sure. After all, part of being a good spy is making sure nobody knows you are one.

PRINCE WHIPPLE

BORN: 1750, ANOMABO, GHANA | DIED: 1796, PORTSMOUTH, NEW HAMPSHIRE

From Wealth to Slavery to Freedom

Prince Whipple was born in Africa. When he was about ten years old, his wealthy parents sent him to America to be educated. However, he was kidnapped by a slave trader and eventually sold to William Whipple of New Hampshire as a house slave. When the Revolution started, William Whipple was made a captain in the Continental Army and took Prince as his bodyguard. In 1777, William was promoted to brigadier general and sent to Vermont. Prince joined him but demanded his freedom, saying, "You are going to fight for your liberty, but I have none to fight for." William agreed—if Prince stayed in the military. Prince consented and, according to the Portsmouth, New Hampshire, town records, General Whipple granted Prince the rights of a freeman on February 22, 1781—Prince's wedding day.

ARTISTIC MYSTERY

Traditionally, the Black man near Washington's knee in Washington Crossing the Delaware, *painted in 1851, was supposedly Prince Whipple. But neither General Whipple nor Prince Whipple was actually near Trenton at the time.*

PRINCE ESTABROOK

BORN: CIRCA 1741, MASSACHUSETTS | DIED: 1830, ASHBY, MASSACHUSETTS

The First Black Man to Fight in the Revolution

Prince Estabrook was an enslaved Black man owned by Benjamin Estabrook of Lexington, Massachusetts, in 1775. When 700 British troops marched to Concord, Prince Estabrook volunteered to fight. A skirmish broke out—the famous Battle of Lexington and Concord*—and Prince was wounded in the shoulder. He fully recovered and was soon back in action, serving at the Battle of Bunker Hill and later at Fort Ticonderoga. After the war, Estabrook returned to Lexington as a free man, thanks to the Quock Walker case, in which it was declared, using the words of the new 1780 Massachusetts constitution, that "all men were born free and equal." As a free man, Prince remained with Estabrook's family and continued to live and work on the farm.

*SEVENTY-NINE OTHER ORDINARY MEN—FARMERS, COOPERS, COBBLERS, CABINETMAKERS—ALSO RISKED THEIR LIVES AND EVERYTHING THEY OWNED TO BE PART OF THIS CONFRONTATION. WHEN "THE SHOT THAT WAS HEARD AROUND THE WORLD" WAS FIRED, IT WAS THESE FORGOTTEN FOUNDERS—NOT THE ARISTOCRATS OR THE INTELLECTUALS—WHO WERE THERE.

THINK DEEPER

Read about the artistic mystery to the left. Why do you think the artist included Prince Whipple, even though he wasn't actually there?

HONOR OVERDUE

The town of Lexington honored Prince Estabrook with a monument in front of Buckman Tavern in 2008. The inscription can be read to the right.

IN HONOR OF PRINCE ESTABROOK:

Prince Estabrook was a slave who lived in Lexington. At dawn on April 19, קדךר, he was one of the Lexington Minute Men awaiting the arrival of the British Regulars at the Buckman Tavern. In the battle that followed, Prince Estabrook was wounded on Lexington Green. Through circumstances and destiny, he thus became the first Black soldier to fight in the American Revolution. This monument is dedicated to the memory of Prince Estabrook and the thousands of other courageous Black patriots long denied the recognition they deserve.

THE FIRST RHODE ISLAND REGIMENT

FORMED: MAY 1775 | REORGANIZED: JANUARY 1781 | DISBANDED: DECEMBER 1783

The First Black Battalion

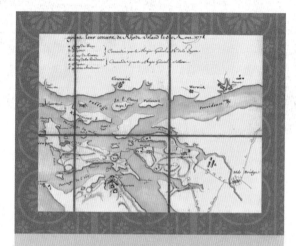

The First Rhode Island Regiment became known as the first Black battalion in US military history. Even though there were Native Americans and white men in the regiment (in fact, all the officers were white), it was called the "Black Regiment" because of the large number of Black soldiers in its ranks.*

Though small, the First Rhode Island Regiment had a big impact. In the Battle of Rhode Island, while fighting for the first time alongside French soldiers, the regiment drove back three Hessian** regiments of the British army. The regiment's courageous performance led to more African Americans enlisting in the Continental Army. Next, the regiment fought in the Hudson River Valley in New York against the British Loyalist militia, called "cowboys," who stole cattle from local farmers and sold them to the British Army in New York City. Later, they helped defend Fort Mercer at the Battle of Red Bank in New Jersey, and finally took part in Yorktown in the last battle of the war.

On January 1, 1781, the First Regiment was consolidated with the Second Regiment and renamed the Rhode Island Regiment. When the Rhode Island Regiment veterans were finally discharged at Saratoga, New York, it was one of the few units in the Continental Army to have served throughout the entire seven years of the war.

*THE REGIMENT EVENTUALLY TOTALED ABOUT 225 MEN; ABOUT 140 OF THESE WERE LIKELY BLACK.

**HESSIANS WERE PROFESSIONAL GERMAN SOLDIERS PAID TO FIGHT FOR THE BRITISH.

A SEVEN-YEAR FIGHT

Soldiers from the First Rhode Island Regiment participated in the Revolution from beginning to end, including:

- *Siege of Boston*
- *Battle of Bunker Hill*
- *Battle of Long Island*
- *Battle of Harlem Heights*
- *Battle of White Plains*
- *Battle of Trenton*
- *Battle of Princeton*
- *Battle of Red Bank*
- *Siege of Fort Mifflin*
- *Valley Forge*
- *Battle of Rhode Island (depicted in the map above)*
- *Battle of Pine's Bridge*
- *Siege and Battle of Yorktown*

THINK DEEPER

Though mostly Black, the regiment did include whites. Black and white soldiers wouldn't be integrated again until World War II, over 150 years later. What happened? Why do you think it took so long?

PENSION PROBLEMS

Though it wasn't uncommon for veterans of the Revolutionary War to have difficulty getting the pensions and land they were promised for fighting, it was often even harder for Black veterans. In 1784, a group of veterans from the Rhode Island Regiment hired an attorney to get back pay from the US War Department. As a result, the Rhode Island Assembly passed legislation requiring local townships to care for all veterans of color.

CHERISHED COLORS

The flag of the Rhode Island Battalion—a unit's flag is officially called its "colors"—was presented to the Rhode Island Assembly in 1784 and has been in the state house ever since.

UNIFORMS OF THE REVOLUTIONARY WAR

At the time of the American Revolution, uniforms were essential so that soldiers didn't shoot people who were on their own side. Often, uniforms also showed a person's rank.

REDCOATS

British soldiers wore bright red uniforms, so they were often called "redcoats." The colonists had different names for them: "bloody backs" or "lobsters"—a fitting insult, since lobsters at the time were considered low-life peasant food and even used as fertilizer. Interestingly, the term "lobster back" didn't show up in print until several decades after the war.

BLUECOATS

Early in the war, many American soldiers wore long, brown coats (see B in illustration on opposite page). In 1779, however, George Washington ordered the Continental Army to wear blue coats and white vests. Blue was picked to make the uniforms clearly different from the red ones of the British. Each state had different colors for the linings, buttons, and facings. New Hampshire, Rhode Island (see A), Connecticut, and Massachusetts used white; New York and New Jersey used buff (tan); Pennsylvania, Delaware, Maryland, and Virginia used red; North Carolina, South Carolina, and Georgia soldiers used blue.

TRICORNE HATS

Also called cocked hats, tricorne hats were the height of fashion during the 1700s. Because the edges were turned up and pinned down, tricorne hats allowed men to show off their wigs (and thus their social status).

GREENCOATS

Loyalist regiments like the New Jersey Volunteers (called "Skinner's Greens") wore green coats.

HESSIANS

Hessians were German soldiers paid to fight for the British. They wore blue coats with colored facings.

FRENCH

America's French allies (see C) wore white uniforms with jackets and coats in various shades of blue.

COCKADES

A cockade was an ornament on a hat (see 1796 French example to the right). When the Continental Army had no uniforms, cockades were used to show their rank. Field officers wore pink cockades, captains wore white or buff, and lower ranks wore green.

A sampling of Revolutionary War uniforms as painted by Jean Baptiste Antoine de Verger, a French artist who fought in the war with America's French allies

ABIGAIL ADAMS

BORN: 1744, WEYMOUTH, MASSACHUSETTS | DIED: 1818, QUINCY, MASSACHUSETTS

Her Husband Was President. Her Son Was President. She May Have Been the Smartest of the Three.

Abigail was born in 1744. Though she was largely deprived of a formal education, her mother taught her to read and write, and Abigail instructed herself in literature with books from her father's vast library. Abigail married John Adams in 1764, and their close, trusting relationship is still talked about today. During John's time serving in the Continental Congress, Abigail sent countless letters discussing policy, government, and the war. She was John's closest confidant throughout his life and was so involved in politics during his time as president that some called her "Mrs. President."

Abigail was a champion of women's rights and, indeed, all human rights. And she wasn't shy about letting people know what she thought. Here are a few notable quotes from Abigail's letters to her husband, John. As Abigail put it, "My bursting heart must find vent at my pen."

FROM ABIGAIL'S PEN:

ON WOMEN

"I long to hear that you have declared an independency . . . in the new code of laws . . . remember the ladies. [We] will not hold ourselves bound by any laws in which we have no voice or representation."

"If we mean to have Heroes, Statesmen, and Philosophers, we should have learned women."

ON NEVER GIVING UP

Abigail's words of encouragement were especially important to her husband, John (pictured above), who was working in Congress to pass the Declaration of Independence and felt frustrated.

"It is not in the still calm of life, or the repose of a pacific station, that great characters are formed."

"It's never too late to get back on your feet . . . make sure you accomplish what you were put here for."

"A people fired . . . with love of their country and of liberty . . . will not be disheartened or dispirited by a succession of unfortunate events. But like them, may we learn by defeat the power of becoming invincible."

THINK DEEPER

John Adams leaned heavily on Abigail for political insight and optimistic support in the face of enormous danger and uncertainty. John would become a leading voice for the cause of independence and the architect behind the Declaration of Independence. Imagine for a moment that Abigail wasn't in the picture. Would history have been different without her?

ON EDUCATION

"Learning is not attained by chance; it must be sought for with ardor and attended to with diligence."

"I've always felt that a person's intelligence is directly reflected by the number of conflicting points of view he can entertain simultaneously on the same topic."

ON LIVING RIGHT

"To be good, and do good, is the whole duty of man comprised in a few words."

PHILLIS WHEATLEY

BORN: CIRCA 1753, SENEGAL, AFRICA | DIED: 1784, BOSTON, MASSACHUSETTS

The Mother of African American Literature

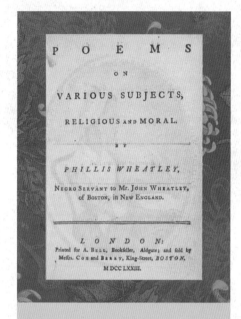

One of America's first great writers was an enslaved woman from Massachusetts: Phillis Wheatley. Born in Senegal, West Africa, Wheatley was sold into slavery as a child and purchased as a house servant by a Boston merchant named John Wheatley. Her name, "Phillis," came from the name of the ship she was transported on.

Recognizing that Phillis had an excellent mind, the Wheatleys taught her to read and write but forbade her from interacting with the other slaves in the family. By the time she was twelve, Phillis could read and write not only English but Greek and Latin as well. She studied ancient Greek and Roman writers in addition to those of the Enlightenment.*

When she was fourteen, Phillis wrote her first poem. But it took some convincing for many colonists to believe that a Black could write such a work. In 1772, Phillis had to defend herself as the author of her poems in court. Fortunately, the court sided with her and the question of authorship was settled.

In 1773, Phillis's first book, *Poems on Various Subjects*, was published in London. Even the great French philosopher Voltaire was impressed by her compositions, and the Wheatleys granted Phillis her freedom shortly after its publication.

As hostility grew between Great Britain and her colonies, Phillis started writing about politics and, to some extent, slavery, perhaps hoping that the war would bring about freedom for all slaves in America. Famously, during the Siege of Boston in 1775, she wrote the poem *To His Excellency George Washington*, which praised Washington and the American Revolution as a noble cause. After she had it sent to Washington at his Cambridge headquarters, Washington wrote back, saying, "However undeserving I may be of such encomium**, the style

CRITICAL ACCLAIM

Many luminaries of her time praised Phillis's works of poetry.

"Phillis, the African favorite of the Nine [muses] and Apollo." —John Paul Jones

"When we consider them as the productions of a young, untutored African, who wrote them after six months careful study of the English language, we cannot but suppress our admiration for talents so vigorous and lively." —Selina Hastings, Countess of Huntingdon

THINK DEEPER

At first, many colonists didn't believe Phillis could have written her poems. Why do you think they felt that way? Have you ever felt that way about another person? Where do you think those feelings come from?

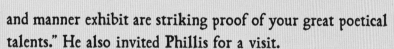

and manner exhibit are striking proof of your great poetical talents." He also invited Phillis for a visit.

In 1778, after the Wheatleys died, Phillis married John Peters, a free Black. Life was not easy, however, and after her husband was imprisoned for debt, Phillis had to work as a boarding house maid. Sadly, hardship and illness took a heavy toll on the young writer, and Phillis died at the age of thirty-one, not long after giving birth.

One can only wonder what more Phillis's pen might have contributed to a nation wrestling with race and equality after the Revolution. Her brilliance and literary talent made her an international hero, and today, Phillis is still regarded as the mother of African American literature.

*THE ENGLIGHTENMENT WAS A EUROPEAN INTELLECTUAL MOVEMENT OF THE LATE SEVENTEENTH AND EIGHTEENTH CENTURIES EMPHASIZING REASON AND INDIVIDUALISM RATHER THAN TRADITION AND RELIGION.

**ENCOMIUM MEANS "PRAISE."

PHILLIS'S POEM

Thee, first in peace and honours,—we demand
The grace and glory of thy martial band.

[. . .]

Proceed, great chief, with virtue on thy side,
Thy ev'ry action let the goddess guide.
A crown, a mansion, and a throne that shine,
With gold unfading, *WASHINGTON!* be thine.

PETER SALEM

BORN: 1750, FRAMINGHAM, MASSACHUSETTS | DIED: 1816, FRAMINGHAM, MASSACHUSETTS

Hero of the Battle of Bunker Hill (Really, Breed's Hill)

Born into slavery, Peter Salem was given his freedom when he enlisted in the Patriot militia. Fighting alongside other Black minutemen, Peter was at the very first battles in Lexington and Concord. Most famously, he was also at the Battle of Bunker Hill,* the first big battle of the war, and is thought to have fired the shot that killed the British leader, Major Pitcairn. An eyewitness, Aaron White of Connecticut, later wrote that as Major Pitcairn was waving his sword and commanding the rebels to surrender, "a Negro soldier stepped forward and, aiming his musket at the major's bosom, blew him through." Even though they lost, the Patriots proved they could go toe-to-toe with the world's most powerful army—which had twice as many casualties as the Americans and lost many officers. The news of Pitcairn's death spread excitement throughout all the colonies and generated support for the American cause.

Throughout the rest of the war, Peter served with the 4th Continental Regiment in the battles of Harlem Heights, Trenton, Saratoga, Monmouth, and Stony Point.

Famous artist John Trumbull included Peter in his 1786 painting of Bunker Hill. In 1882, the people of Framingham erected a monument to honor Salem's service in the Revolutionary War. And later, the Daughters of the American Revolution made Salem's home in Leicester a historical monument.

*ACTUALLY, THE BATTLE OF BUNKER HILL WAS FOUGHT ON BREED'S HILL, WHICH IS ACROSS THE CHARLES RIVER FROM BUNKER HILL.

BATTLE HERO

Out of approximately one thousand Patriots who fought at the Battle of Bunker Hill (shown above), between 35 and 150 were Black. Peter Salem is shown here in the detail below.

QUICK FIGHTERS

Some colonial militias called themselves "minutemen" because they could be ready to fight at a minute's notice.

At first, the British under-estimated the colonists, and they suffered heavy casualties at the Battle of Bunker Hill. What motivated the colonists to fight? What about the British? Can that make a difference? Why or why not?

NATIVE AMERICANS AND THE REVOLUTION

Tough Choices

Most Native American tribes saw the Revolutionary War as a "family feud" between the King of England and his subjects and tried to stay neutral. Of those who did get involved, deciding which side to go with frequently split tribes in two or estranged them from neighboring tribes. Both the British and the Patriots tried hard to convince Native Americans to join their side; officers in both armies, including George Washington, had fought in the French and Indian War and knew the value of Native American warriors as scouts and fighting men.

Support for the British

Most Native Americans supported the British in hopes that they would stop colonial expansion into their lands in the West, as they had with the Royal Proclamation of 1763. They believed the British would keep the boundary the same.

Support for the Patriots

There were, however, some Native Americans who did support the colonists. The first to do so was the Mohican tribe

CROSSING THE LINE

After the French and Indian War, the British agreed to stop colonial expansion past a certain point westward (pictured on the map above) as part of the Royal Proclamation of 1763. Many Native Americans feared that if the Patriots won the Revolution, they would cross the line and keep colonizing west. Their fears were correct.

from Stockbridge, Massachusetts, who sent men to join the Patriot militia in Boston in 1775 and also fought at Bunker Hill. Of even greater importance to the colonists, the Stockbridge-Mohicans were ambassadors to other Indigenous nations, including the large Iroquois Confederacy of six nations, from which the Abenaki, the Delaware, and the Shawnee eventually joined Washington's forces in Valley Forge. Soon thereafter, the Micmac and Maliseet formed an alliance with the colonists when they signed the Treaty of Watertown, the first foreign treaty after the Declaration of Independence. The Catawba nation (North Carolina), the Creek and Yuchi (throughout the Southeast), and others also allied with the colonists.

Defeat Even in Victory

In the end, while the Revolutionary War cost Britain the Thirteen Colonies, it cost Native Americans much more. In the Treaty of Paris, the British gave the new nation all the territory east of the Mississippi and south of Canada—land that had traditionally belonged to Native American tribes—without even considering what Native Americans thought, needed, or wanted. Even the Stockbridge-Mohicans discovered that they were not only excluded from the new republic, but even the memory of their services was forgotten or purged from the record. The only recognition they ever received was a "Certificate to the Muhhekunnuk Indians" from George Washington, giving "testimony of their attachment to the United States of America during the late war."

JOSEPH BRANT

Born Thayendanegea *(Mohawk for "he places two bets together"), Joseph Brant was perhaps the most prominent Native American leader during the time of the Revolution. He learned math and English, studied classic literature, and met both King George III and George Washington. During the war, he led attacks against the colonists on the New York frontier. After the war, as a result of his people losing their lands, he helped negotiate and create a Mohawk reserve in present-day Ontario.*

THINK DEEPER

The British originally proposed stopping westward expansion in their Royal Proclamation of 1763. But when negotiating peace with America after the war, that was cast aside. Why do you think that happened? How would you feel if you were a tribe who had supported the British? The Americans?

MARY HAYS MCCAULY

BORN: 1754, TRENTON, NEW JERSEY | DIED: 1832, CARLISLE, PENNSYLVANIA

The Real Molly Pitcher

You may have heard about the Revolutionary War hero Molly Pitcher, but you probably never heard of Mary Ludwig Hays McCauly. The trouble is, Molly Pitcher never really existed—but Mary Ludwig Hays McCauley certainly did, and she likely did the things people have long said Molly Pitcher did.

In 1777, Mary, a stout, strong woman, followed her husband, William Hays, to the winter camp at Valley Forge, where he trained as an artilleryman under Baron von Steuben (see Foreign Aid on page 46). William's job was to load the cannon using a ramrod to drive the cannonball down the barrel and pack it tight against the gunpowder. On a hot June day, during the Battle of Monmouth (New Jersey), Mary Hays was carrying pitchers of water to cool the soldiers and the cannon and to soak the rammer rag so it would slide more easily. When Mary saw her husband collapse—either from the heat or from being wounded—she picked up the ramrod and loaded the cannon herself. In fact, she did it all day long! Some say she even fired the cannon. Supposedly, George Washington witnessed her courage and made Mary Hays a noncommissioned officer in the army. Almost immediately, pictures of "Captain Molly" with a cannon were printed in Patriot newspapers.

After the war, Mary Hays went back to work as a domestic servant. In 1822, she asked for a pension for her Revolutionary War service, and the Pennsylvania legislature gave her $40 and annual payments of $40 each.

In 1876, the American Revolution centennial (a one-hundred-year celebration) renewed interest in Mary, and the town of Carlisle, Pennsylvania, built a statue of her that described her as the "Heroine of Monmouth." Molly—that is, Mary—even appeared on a World War II poster that said, "America's women have always fought for freedom."

"PITCHING" IN

Throughout the war, women supported the troops in many ways. They made food, sewed and washed clothing, and nursed the wounded. Often, they brought pitchers of water to keep the men and cannons cool in the heat of battle. This is where the name "Pitcher" came from.

THINK DEEPER

Many legends grew up around the story of Mary, and today, people still mistakenly know her as "Molly Pitcher." Is it possible for historical stories to be wrong? Can wrong stories become myths that motivate people in a good way? How do facts matter?

CLOSE CALL

According to one popular story, Mary was once nearly hit by a musket ball or cannonball that went between her legs and blew away her petticoat. She is said to have reacted by saying, "Well, that could have been worse."

GALLOPING GALLOPERS!

The most common cannon was the three-pound "galloper," although larger cannons could shoot balls of up to eighteen pounds. A crew of ten could fire four times per minute!

EDWARD "NED" HECTOR

BORN: 1744, PENNSYLVANIA | DIED: 1834, NORRISTOWN, PENNSYLVANIA

Brave Bombardier. Fearless Wagoner.

The American army relied on more than just soldiers who shot muskets or used bayonets. There were blacksmiths, cooks, gunsmiths, hostlers (they took care of horses), musket ball makers, quartermasters (they scheduled the movement of troops and organized needed supplies), and wagoners, who drove the wagons that moved troops around and brought them the supplies and food they needed.

Born a free Black man, Ned Hector was both a bombardier (part of an artillery crew that shot cannons) and a wagoner. It was during the Battle of Brandywine, in Pennsylvania, that he showed incredible grit and gumption. When the Patriots were being overrun, Ned's commanding officer gave the order to abandon everything, retreat, and "save yourself." Ned famously replied, "The enemy shall not have my team; I will save my horses and myself!"

Picking up the rifles that had been tossed away, Ned threw them in his wagon and escaped under fire from the British—saving his wagon, his horses, and the weapons, which would be desperately needed by the Patriots in coming battles. According to one account, Ned "showed great courage . . . when he refused to let his team and wagon fall into enemy hands." This was entirely the opposite of Hector's commanding officer, who was later put on trial for leaving the battle in an "un-officer-like" way.

In recognition of his bravery, a street in the town where he lived was named Hector Street in 1850. Later, in 1976, a historical plaque was erected at the intersection of Hector and Fayette Street honoring Ned and the many African Americans who served during the American Revolution.

FREE BLACKS

Though the vast majority of Blacks in colonial America were slaves or indentured servants, there were some free Blacks in the colonies from the very beginning. Free Blacks had access to the justice system and appeared to be treated (generally) equally by the courts. By the Civil War some seventy years later, thanks in some measure to the rise of Southern agriculture, slavery had become fully institutionalized in the American South, and limited freedom for Blacks came to dominate much of American culture.

THINK DEEPER

Ned showed incredible courage. Why do you think he acted that way? Why do you think his commanding officer didn't?

THE "WHEEL" DEALS

Someone who made and repaired wooden wheels was called a "wheelwright." Someone who drove wagons was called a "wagoner." Both were essential jobs during colonial days, especially for an army constantly on the move.

BETSY ROSS

BORN: 1752, GLOUCESTER CITY, NEW JERSEY | DIED: 1836, PHILADELPHIA, PENNSYLVANIA

She Made More than Just a Flag

You could hardly say Betsy Ross is forgotten. How many people have songs about their sewing ability that have survived over a century? (See partial lyrics on opposite page.) While Betsy has become almost an unreal, mythical figure, here are a few things we know about her real life.

Elizabeth "Betsy" Griscom was born into a large family (one of seventeen children!) and taught how to sew by her great-aunt. Since she lived in Philadelphia, which was the capital of the Continental Congress from 1774 to 1783, she knew many influential Americans, including George Washington, who went to the same church.

During the Revolution, Betsy was kept busy supporting the Continental Army. She repaired uniforms, made tents and blankets, and even stuffed paper tube cartridges with musket balls for ammunition. And yes, she also made flags and banners, primarily for the Pennsylvania Navy. One of those flags is now considered to be the possible inspiration for the American "Betsy Ross Flag."

While Betsy sewed this flag, it's not clear whether she actually designed it. Some historians think the design was created by Francis Hopkinson, a member of the Continental Congress and signer of the Declaration of Independence. He also designed Continental paper money and was the only person to submit a bill to Congress asking to be paid for his designs.

In fact, the story of her making the first American flag wasn't even talked about until 1870, nearly fifty years after her passing, when Ross's grandson presented a research paper to the Historical Society of Pennsylvania and claimed that his grandmother had "made with her hands the first flag" of the United States. Like a lot of historical things, the truth is that we'll probably never know for sure what happened, but there's no doubt that Betsy's support for the war effort and patriotism shaped the nation she loved.

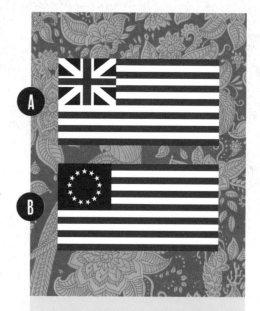

OLD GLORY

The first unofficial national flag was the Grand Union Flag (A) raised by Washington near his headquarters outside Boston, Massachusetts, on January 1, 1776. In the upper-left corner, there was still the emblem of the British flag. The first official flag, known as Old Glory or the Stars and Stripes (B), was approved by the Continental Congress in 1777. The emblem of the British Union Flag was replaced by thirteen white stars on a blue background, representing the thirteen colonies.

THINK DEEPER

Betsy supported the war in many ways. Why do you think she's mostly remembered for sewing the flag?

"HOW BETSY MADE THE FLAG"

Said Washington to Betsy Ross, "A flag our nation needs,
To lead our valiant soldiers on to high and noble deeds;
Now, can you make one for us?" To which she made reply
"I am not certain that I can; at least I'll gladly try."
So she took some red for the blood they shed,
Some white for purity,
Some stars so bright from the sky o'erhead,
Some blue for loyalty,
And sewed them all together,
For loyal hearts and true;
And hand in hand as one we stand,
For the red, white and blue.

Though its accuracy is doubtful, the song "How Betsy Made the Flag," written in 1915, is still sung today.

SEW SIMPLE

Betsy supposedly changed the stars from six-pointed to five-pointed, telling George Washington that five-pointed stars were easier to make.

45

 t's easy to forget that the United States wouldn't be a country today if it hadn't been for foreign people and countries who helped them defeat the strongest military force in the world. From Germany to France, Poland to Ireland, here are a few of those heroes and a brief description of what they did.

MARQUIS DE LA FAYETTE, FRANCE

Marie-Joseph Paul Yves Roch Gilbert du Motier, known simply (and thankfully) as just the Marquis de La Fayette in the United States, entered the military at age thirteen, following his family's tradition. Convinced that the American Revolution was noble and right, he traveled to America and was made a major general at age nineteen. Injured at Brandywine, he served with distinction in the Battle of Rhode Island, then sailed home to get more money and aid from the French. In 1781, his troops blocked the British at Yorktown and helped win the last major battle of the war.

BARON VON STEUBEN, PRUSSIA (GERMANY)

Friedrich Wilhelm August Heinrich Ferdinand von Steuben (phew . . . those looooong European names!) was an officer in the Prussian army who was an ardent supporter of the American cause. Recommended by Ben Franklin, he trained the disorganized Continental Army and turned it into a serious fighting force during the winter of 1777 at Valley Forge, Pennsylvania. (For instance, Americans had previously used bayonets mainly as cooking skewers or tools. Von Steuben showed them how to use them as weapons.) He also organized camps so that the latrines (bathrooms) were far from the kitchens and much more sanitary. And he made the army keep accurate records of all the money spent and wrote *Regulations for the Order and Discipline of the Troops of the United States*, a manual that was used as the country's military guide until 1812.

HERCULES MULLIGAN, IRELAND

Born in Ireland, Hercules came to New York City when he was six years old. A passionate patriot who roomed with Alexander Hamilton, Hercules stole British cannons and tore down a statue of King George III while a member of the Sons of Liberty. As a tailor who worked for British officers, he often figured out the British army's moves by asking his clients when they'd need their uniforms back! Twice, this information was delivered on horseback to the Continental Army by his slave, Cato Howe, who had enlisted in the army along with Hercules. Both times, these messages kept George Washington from being killed or captured. After the war, Cato was freed and became a farmer; Mulligan kept working as a tailor until age eighty and was a founding member of an early abolitionist society.

Other countries were essential to America's founding. How did they make a difference? Can they still make a difference today? How?

ADMIRAL DE GRASSE AND COMTE DE ROCHAMBEAU, FRANCE

The decision that ended the Revolutionary War was not made by Washington but by the French Admiral Francois Joseph Paul de Grasse (A) and the head of the French army in the colonies, Comte de Rochambeau (B). Washington wanted to attack the British in New York City, but Rochambeau, who had a small army, wanted to face the British at Yorktown, Virginia. De Grasse sided with Rochambeau. Consequently, the French fleet fought the British off Chesapeake Bay in the Battle of the Virginia Capes. After both sides had blasted away at each other for hours, the British fleet was severely damaged and decided to sail to New York for repairs. This left the British army at Yorktown surrounded on both land and sea, and it quickly surrendered, effectively ending the war and British rule over the colonies.

TADEUSZ KOSCIUSZKO, POLAND

Andrzej Tadeusz Bonawentura Kosciuszko was a Polish-Lithuanian military engineer, statesman, and military leader. Sympathetic to the American cause and an advocate of human rights, he sailed to America in 1776 and was made a colonel in the Continental Army. An accomplished military architect, he designed and oversaw the construction of state-of-the-art fortifications like the fort that kept the British from sailing up the Delaware River to Philadelphia, a defense plan that stopped the British cold and forced them to surrender at Saratoga, and the defenses of West Point. Later, upon his death, Kosciuszko authorized Thomas Jefferson to use his money to purchase the freedom of slaves and provide them with an education.

FILIPPO MAZZEI, ITALY

Born in Italy, the writer and political activist Filippo "Philip" Mazzei became a supporter of the American cause after moving to Virginia in 1773. As a close friend of Thomas Jefferson, Mazzei frequently spent time with Jefferson sharing ideas. Jefferson, in fact, gave Mazzei credit for coming up with the most famous line in the Declaration of Independence: "all men are created equal." The words first appeared in Italian in Mazzei's essay *Furioso* as *tutti gli uomini sono per natura egualmente liberi e indipenti*—"all men are by nature equally free and independent." Mazzei was given an original copy of the Declaration by Jefferson himself.

THOMAS TOWNSHEND, JAMES BOSWELL, WILLIAM PITT; ENGLAND

Many British people in England did not support the war. Thomas Townshend (C), an important member of the House of Commons, said that "the Government and Majority have drawn us into a war, that in our opinion is unjust in its Principle and ruinous in its consequences." Later, the famous diarist James Boswell (D) wrote that "those who could understand were against the American war, as almost every man is now." And William Pitt (E), son of England's former prime minister, argued that "the expense of it has been enormous . . . and yet what has the British nation received in return? Nothing but a series of ineffective victories or severe defeats." Though King George III wanted to keep the colonies in the British empire and kept the war going until 1783 (seven years!), this opposition certainly helped bring it to an end.

JAMES ROBINSON

BORN: 1753, EASTERN SHORE, MARYLAND | DIED: 1868, DETROIT, MICHIGAN

The Most Decorated African American of the War

James Robinson's owner, Francis de Shields, had him enlist and fight for the Patriots with the promise that he could earn his freedom. As part of one of several African American regiments commanded by the Marquis de Lafayette, Robinson fought in at least seven battles, including Yorktown, where he led the charge against a British rampart (wall) and defeated three British soldiers at once. Lafayette was so impressed that he personally awarded Robinson a Gold Medal of Valor, making him the highest-decorated African American veteran of the Revolutionary War. But after the war, when de Shields died, his heirs forced Robinson back into slavery. Later, in the War of 1812, Robinson enlisted again at age sixty-one and fought valiantly in the Battle of New Orleans. But he was, once again, returned to slavery when the battle was over. It took until the 1830s for him to finally gain his freedom, after which he lived to the incredible age of 115!

On June 22, 2019, a military funeral was held by the Michigan societies of the Sons of the American Revolution, the General Society of the War of 1812, and the American Legion—151 years after Robinson's death.

A RARE HONOR

Medals (some from during and after the war are pictured above) were rarely given out during the Revolutionary War, making Robinson particularly exceptional.

19

WILLIAM FLORA

BORN: 1755, PORTSMOUTH, VIRGINIA | DIED: 1818, PHILADELPHIA, PENNSYLVANIA

Hero of the Battle of Great Bridge

Born to free Black parents, William Flora joined the Patriot cause when Lord Dunmore, the royal governor of Virginia, tried to dissolve the Virginia House of Burgesses (the colony's elected representatives) and not let the Patriot militias have guns, powder, and shot.*

> THINK DEEPER
>
> *James's owner freed him, but his owner's heirs forced James back into slavery. Why would they do that? Does that seem fair to you?*

On December 8, 1775, at the Battle of Great Bridge, William was a lookout on the narrow bridge surrounded by the impassable Great Dismal Swamp. When the British charged, Flora fought against a whole platoon all by himself, firing eight rapid shots. Then Flora removed boards from the bridge, which stopped the British from following the Patriots and gave the Patriots time to get organized and finally beat the British. Even though the battle lasted less than an hour, the British lost more than one hundred men, killed and wounded, while only one Patriot was wounded. Shortly thereafter, when the Patriots entered the city of Norfolk, Lord Dunmore and many Tories (Loyalists who supported the British) fled Virginia.

After the battle, Flora's bravery was praised by his fellow soldiers, newspapers, and his commanding officer. Importantly, Virginia finally joined the war, which at this point had been happening mainly in New England. Today, on a preserved battleground, there is now a historical marker honoring William Flora and other Patriots.

*PATRICK HENRY FAMOUSLY RESPONDED TO DUNMORE BY SAYING "GIVE ME LIBERTY, OR GIVE ME DEATH."

20

SARAH FRANKLIN BACHE

BORN: 1743, PHILADELPHIA, PENNSYLVANIA | DIED: 1808, PHILADELPHIA, PENNSYLVANIA

A House Divided

Her father was Ben Franklin. Her half-brother was the Loyalist governor of New Jersey. And Sarah was a passionate Patriot.

So just imagine what Sunday dinner at her house was like! Truthfully, conflict like this was common in many colonial families and towns. Vehement disagreement about whether the Revolution was a good (or bad) thing filled daily discussions in the American colonies.

From the beginning, Sarah made up her mind to support Independence and became a significant contributor to the cause. Often collaborating with Ben as a hostess of political meetings, Sarah raised sorely needed money for the Continental Army. She also organized a group that made 2,200 shirts for the raggedly clothed soldiers at Valley Forge. Despite fierce opposition from her half-brother, William, and even though she and her family were twice forced to evacuate their home in Philadelphia when the British took over the city, Sarah always remained devoted to the revolutionary cause.

Though she had a complicated relationship with her father, Sarah was also devoted to him and took care of him until he died in 1790. In the end, Franklin left most of his estate to Sarah and nothing, except some worthless land in Nova Scotia, to William.

BENJAMIN FRANKLIN

Ben Franklin was a writer, diplomat, politician, scientist, philosopher, composer, and inventor. As a scientist, he was a major figure in the history of physics for his discoveries and theories about electricity. As an inventor, he created the lightning rod, bifocals, Franklin stove, and glass harmonica. He started Philadelphia's first fire department, public lending library, and the University of Pennsylvania and earned the title "The First American" for his early, tireless campaign to bring the colonies together.

WILLIAM FRANKLIN

As the last British Governor of New Jersey (1763-1776) William secretly reported Patriot activities to London. On January 13, 1775, he urged the New Jersey Legislature to take the road toward prosperity as a part of England rather than a road to civil war and anarchy. Instead, the legislature unanimously passed a resolution to support the radical Patriots in Boston.

THINK DEEPER

How can families who strongly disagree on issues discuss them calmly, honestly, and in a friendly way?

THE OTHER BATTLEFRONT

Sarah's letters to her father provide important details about the difficulties of life for colonists at home during the war. The first excerpt to the right is about her family's evacuation from Philadelphia; the second is about the extreme cost of goods during the war.

ESCAPE!

"There was such confusion that it was a hard matter to get out [of Philadelphia] at any rate; when we shall get back again I know not." (1776)

INFLATION

"There is hardly such a thing as living in town, everything is so high. If I was to mention the prices of the common necessaries of life, they would astonish you . . . They really ask me six dollars for a pair of gloves, and I have been obliged to pay fifteen pounds for a common calamanco petticoat without quilting that I once could have got for fifteen shillings." (1778)

21

CRISPUS ATTUCKS

BORN: CIRCA 1723, FRAMINGHAM, MASSACHUSETTS | DIED: 1770, BOSTON, MASSACHUSETTS

First American Martyr

The first person killed in the American Revolution was Crispus Attucks.* A man of mixed heritage—African and Native American (his mother was from the Natick branch of the Wampanoag tribe)—Crispus worked as a sailor on a whaling ship. On March 5, 1770, when his ship was in Boston, he became part of an angry Patriot mob throwing stones, clubs, snowballs, and ice at the British soldier guarding the Customs House, where taxes were collected. When the soldier called for help, he was joined by other British soldiers. Then someone—and no one really knows who—yelled, "Fire!" The British opened fire and five men fell dead. The first was Crispus Attucks, with two musket balls in his chest.

A large funeral was held in Boston, and the five victims of what came to be called the Boston Massacre were buried together in Boston's Old Granary Burying Ground. In the 1800s, supporters of the abolitionist movement praised Crispus for playing a heroic role in the founding of the United States.

Over the years, Crispus Attucks has been featured on postage stamps from several countries, including Grenada, Nevis Anguilla, and the United States. Today, on the Boston Common, you can see a monument with a figure representing the Spirit of the Revolution and the names of the five men killed: Crispus Attucks, James Caldwell, Patrick Carr, Samuel Gray, and Samuel Maverick.

*THE NAME ATTUCKS WAS COMMON AMONG NATIVE AMERICANS IN MASSACHUSETTS. IT'S A VERSION OF THE ALGONQUIN/ WAMPANOAG WORD *AHTUQ ES*, MEANING "LITTLE DEAR."

ENGRAVING HISTORY

Two years after the event, John Adams's cousin, Samuel Adams, called it the "Boston Massacre," and Boston artist Henry Pelham made an engraving showing Crispus Attucks getting shot. This picture was copied by Paul Revere, and it cemented the event in American minds as a one-sided tragedy, even though historians still don't know who exactly started it.

THINK DEEPER

John Adams chose to defend the British soldiers—America's enemies—in court. What do you think of that decision?

LAID TO REST

The victims of the Boston Massacre were buried together in Boston's Old Granary Burying Ground. They're in good company: also buried there are Benjamin Franklin's parents, Samuel Adams, John Hancock, Paul Revere, and many others.

PATRIOT DEFENDER

Believing that everyone deserved a fair trial—and in an effort to show the British that the colonies could conduct one—John Adams, a dedicated Patriot and future president of the United States, defended the British soldiers involved in the Boston Massacre. Six were acquitted. Two were found guilty of manslaughter.

22

DEBORAH SAMPSON

BORN: 1760, PLYMPTON, MASSACHUSETTS | DIED: 1827, SHARON, MASSACHUSETTS

A Strong Woman.
A Secret Soldier.

Wanting to be part of the American army, Deborah Sampson tried to enlist twice. The first time, she was discovered to be a woman and turned away. (It was, in fact, a scandal.) But in 1782, when she was twenty-one, Deborah again disguised herself as a man, used her brother's name, Robert Shirtliff, and successfully enlisted in the 4th Massachusetts Regiment. She served for seventeen months. During that time, she fought in several skirmishes and was injured many times. Once, near New York City, she was gashed in the head by a sword and hit with two bullets in her thigh. Not wanting anyone to discover she was a woman, she let doctors treat her head wound but then slipped out of the field hospital, dug one of the bullets out of her leg with a penknife, and closed the wound herself with a sewing needle! She couldn't get the other bullet out—it was in too deep—and her leg never fully healed.

After serving, Deborah was honorably discharged, returned to Massachusetts, married, and had four children. In 1797, a newspaper publisher wrote about Deborah's wartime experiences in *The Female Review: or, Memoirs of an American Young Lady.* In 1802, Deborah embarked on a yearlong tour, delivering lectures about her sensational experiences as a soldier, often in a full military uniform.

Deborah was the only woman to earn a full military pension for participation in the Revolutionary War—though she had to fight hard to get it. There are now statues of her at the library in Sharon, Massachusetts, and at George Washington's home in Virginia.

IDENTITY PROTECTED

Near the end of the war, Deborah became ill while stationed in Philadelphia. The doctor that cared for her discovered that she was a woman. Rather than report her, he took her home, where his wife and a nurse helped care for her in secret.

THINK DEEPER

In 2021, a new law was passed to provide better access to care and benefits for female US veterans. It was named the Deborah Sampson Act. Why do you think that was?

CLEVER DISGUISE

After failing to enlist the first time, Deborah tried enlisting again—this time in a light infantry company. These were considered more elite units than those of average foot soldiers, and the strategy worked: no one ever guessed that a woman could go toe-to-toe with the strongest men!

IN HER OWN WORDS

"I swerved from the accustomed flowery path of female delicacy to walk upon the heroic precipice of feminine perdition! Why can I not fight for my country too?"
—Deborah Sampson

23

BARZILLAI LEW

BORN: 1743 | DIED: 1822

The Fighting Musician

Barzillai Lew's love of music began with his father, Primus. As a free Black man, Primus was a musician who played the fife in the French and Indian War in 1747. Primus's oldest son, Barzillai (pronounced BAR-zeal-ya), often called "Zeal" or "Zelah," followed in his father's footsteps and also became a fifer with the Patriot militia. A large man at six feet tall, Lew was a well-known, talented musician, as well as a cooper (barrel maker) by trade.

At the opening of the American Revolution, Barzillai enlisted in the 27th Regiment from Chelmsford, Massachusetts, and fought at the Battle of Bunker Hill* as a fifer, drummer, and soldier. All during the battle, Barzillai kept American spirits high by playing "There's Nothing Makes the British Run like 'Yankee Doodle Dandy'" on his fife.

In 1777, Lew then went with his regiment to fight at Fort Ticonderoga, New York. Following a decisive Patriot victory there, a fellow soldier wrote this in his diary: "Zeal is selected as a fifer and fiddler for the grand appearance the day . . . [It was] a wonderful show." The "wonderful show" was the surrender of the British to the Patriots at Saratoga—a victory that convinced the French to help the Patriots with soldiers, ships, and money and ultimately helped the Americans win the war.

Following the Revolution, the Lew family played music in towns and cities all over New England. In 1943, musician Duke Ellington wrote a piano piece in Barzillai Lew's honor.

*WHICH WAS REALLY FOUGHT AT BREED'S HILL, REMEMBER.

YANKEE DOODLE

The lyrics of "Yankee Doodle" changed over the years. The song began during the French and Indian War as a British insult toward the Americans, whom they considered uncivilized.

> Yankee Doodle went to town
> A-riding on a pony,
> Stuck a feather in his cap
> And called it macaroni.

"Macaroni" was a term for someone who pretended to be more wealthy and sophisticated than they really were (see 1773 illustrated above). But the Americans turned the song into a defiant anthem and added verses, like this one:

> And there was Cap'n Washington,
> And gentle folks about him;
> They say he's grown so 'tarnal proud
> He will not ride without 'em.

Could you have imagined that music would play such an important role in the army? What talents or abilities do you have? How might they be helpful in a cause that's important to you?

MILITARY MUSIC

A fife is a small, high-pitched wind instrument similar to a piccolo. Fife players, along with drummers, did more than provide entertainment to weary soldiers. They were an important part of communication in an army. The music and beat could signal assembly, alarms, and other commands.

BRITISH PARODY

Of course, the British couldn't let the Americans have all the fun. They created their own version in retaliation:

Yankee Doodle came to town,
For to buy a firelock,
We will tar and feather him,
And so we will John Hancock.

24

LYDIA BARRINGTON DARRAGH

BORN: 1729, DUBLIN, IRELAND | DIED: DECEMBER 28, 1789, PHILADELPHIA, PENNSYLVANIA

The Button Spy

Lydia Barrington Darragh was part of a Quaker family that moved from Dublin, Ireland, to Philadelphia, Pennsylvania, in the 1750s. Since they were Quakers, the Darraghs would not fight; nonetheless, they sided with the Patriots during the American Revolution. During the occupation of Philadelphia by the British, several high-ranking soldiers were quartered* in the Darraghs' home. Additionally, British General Sir William Howe lived across the street and would regularly hold meetings in the Darraghs' house.

Because of this, Lydia saw the chance to help the Patriots. She regularly spied on the soldiers' meetings while bringing them refreshments or firewood. What she found out was then written in a special code and hidden under large, cloth-covered buttons on her son John's coat. John then took the message to his older brother, Charles, who was in the Continental Army.**

On December 2, 1777, the British held a meeting in the Darraghs' house, telling the Darraghs they had to go to bed early that night. Lydia faked being asleep and overheard the soldiers planning a surprise attack on Washington's army in Whitemarsh, Pennsylvania, on December 4th. The next day, Darragh left Philadelphia, saying she had to get flour from a mill outside town. She then met up with a Patriot soldier and handed over the message about the planned assault. This warning gave Washington time to get troops and cannons ready, and consequently, the British did not attack. Darragh's bravery and cunning were crucial in ensuring that this attack at Whitemarsh did not end in a massacre of the American army.

ANN BATES, BRITISH SPY

Women didn't just spy for the Patriots. Many spied for the British too. Ann Bates, a teacher in Philadelphia who was married to a British soldier, disguised herself as a peddler and infiltrated Washington's camp at White Plains, New York. She reported the number of soldiers, guns, cannons, and more to the British general in Philadelphia, who said that "her information . . . was by far superior to every other intelligence." As a result, British General Henry Clinton sent more troops into Rhode Island, forcing the Patriots to flee.

The consequences for being discovered as a spy could have been severe. What do you think gave Lydia the courage to do what she did? Can you find courage like that? How? What would you use it for?

FIGHTING QUAKERS

Quaker beliefs forbid violence. During the American Revolution, Quakers who wanted to fight for the American cause often changed their religion so that they could. Many became Episcopalians.

In 2013, the National Society of the Sons of the American Revolution created the Lydia Darragh Medal to recognize the assistance of the women who work behind the scenes to support their programs.

*AMERICANS WERE FORCED, BY LAW, TO PROVIDE FOOD, DRINK, FUEL, AND TRANSPORTATION TO BRITISH TROOPS, AND EVEN LET THEM LIVE IN THEIR HOUSES. THIS LED TO THE THIRD AMENDMENT OF THE CONSTITUTION, WHICH PREVENTS THE MILITARY FROM FORCING PEOPLE TO HOUSE SOLDIERS.

**FOR FIGHTING IN THE WAR, LYDIA'S SON CHARLES WAS FORCED TO LEAVE THE QUAKERS ON APRIL 27, 1781. LYDIA WAS EXPELLED ON AUGUST 29, 1783.

MORE WOMEN OF COURAGE

During the Revolution, thousands of women pitched in to help the cause. In fact, women were absolutely essential to the success of the war effort. They raised funds, made musket balls, managed homesteads while their husbands fought, and spread patriotic zeal and passion throughout their communities. There are more stories than can possibly fit in this book; here are a few more remarkable heroines:

ANGELICA VROOMAN

When the American army desperately needed ammunition during a battle in 1780, Angelica took an iron spoon and molded bullets for the American troops right in the middle of the field—in the middle of the battle!

PRUDENCE CUMMINGS WRIGHT

When her husband marched away to fight the British, Prudence became captain of a female militia called the "Minutewomen" to protect her hometown of Pepperell, Massachusetts. Dressed as men, the thirty to forty women carried muskets to Jewett's Bridge on the Nashua River, where they stopped the British, captured several soldiers, and intercepted vital dispatches regarding troop movements and the location of hidden Patriot gunpowder. Today, a marker in Pepperell commemorates their courage.

DAUGHTERS OF LIBERTY

To help boycott British goods as a protest of British taxation, the Daughters of Liberty made cloth for colonists to wear (instead of British textiles) and made "liberty tea" from raspberry leaves (instead of imported British tea). One Daughter of Liberty, Sarah Bradlee Fulton, came up with the idea that the Boston Tea Party✱ participants should wear Mohawk disguises and was called the "Mother of the Tea Party." Her thinking helped protect the identity of the participants, and sure enough, only one colonist was ever punished for the act.

MERCY OTIS WARREN

A poet, playwright, and political pamphleteer, Mercy Otis Warren (pictured above) played a critical role in promoting the Patriot cause. She was a frequent correspondent with many early US presidents. In 1805, she wrote the watershed *History of the Rise, Progress, and Termination of the American Revolution.*

MARY HAGIDORN

Disobeying an officer who ordered her to stay in a cellar with the other women and children, Mary shouted, "Captain, I shall not go to that cellar. I will take a spear which I can use as well as any man and help defend the fort." And she did.

GRACE AND RACHEL MARTIN

Hearing that Loyalist soldiers were carrying information that could hurt the Patriots, these sisters used their husbands' clothing to disguise themselves as men, rode into the night, and ambushed the Loyalists. Frightened by these two tough "guys," the Loyalists handed over the papers, and the information never got to the Brits.

MARY NOLES AND ELIZABETH OWEN

After Charleston, South Carolina, fell to the British in 1780, women who were heads of households were forced to swear loyalty to the British. Mary Noles and Elizabeth Owen refused and were banished from the city, along with over 120 other women and 260 children.

*ON DECEMBER 16, 1773, A BAND OF COLONISTS DISGUISED AS NATIVE AMERICANS DESTROYED A SHIPMENT OF BRITISH TEA IN BOSTON HARBOR. CALLED THE "BOSTON TEA PARTY," THIS WAS ONE OF MANY ESCALATING EVENTS THAT LED TO THE REVOLUTION.

Works Cited

"Africa: Global Slavery Index." Global Slavery Index, n.d. https://www.globalslaveryindex.org/2018/findings/regional-analysis/africa/.

"American Indian Biography: Crispus Attucks, Revolutionary War Leader." Native American Netroots, December 6, 2010. http://nativeamericannetroots.net/diary/794.

"The American Revolution." Women & the American Story, February 18, 2021. https://wams.nyhistory.org/settler-colonialism-and-revolution/the-american-revolution/.

"American Spies of the Revolution." George Washington's Mount Vernon, n.d. https://www.mountvernon.org/george-washington/the-revolutionary-war/spying-and-espionage/american-spies-of-the-revolution/.

Apple, Iryna. "Military Women Should Support Deborah Sampson Act." Jewish War Veterans of the U.S.A., December 23, 2019. https://www.jwv.org/military-women-should-support-deborah-sampson-act/.

Ayres, Edward. "African Americans and the American Revolution." Jamestown Settlement and the American Revolution Museum, April 10, 2020. https://jyfmuseums.org/learn/learning-center/colonial-america-american-revolution-learning-resources/american-revolution-essays-timelines-images/african-americans-and-the-american-revolution/.

"Baron Von Steuben." Encyclopædia Britannica. Encyclopædia Britannica, inc., n.d. https://www.britannica.com/biography/Baron-von-Steuben.

Bleyer, Bill. "George Washington's Culper Spy Ring: Separating Fact From Fiction." Journal of the American Revolution, June 3, 2021. https://allthingsliberty.com/2021/06/george-washingtons-culper-spy-ring-separating-fact-from-fiction/.

"Boston Massacre / Crispus Attucks Monument." Crispus Attucks, October 17, 2012. http://www.crispusattucksmuseum.org/boston-massacre-crispus-attucks-monument/#prettyPhoto/.

Brooks, Rebecca Beatrice, et al. "Native Americans in the Revolutionary War." History of Massachusetts Blog, March 7, 2020. https://historyofmassachusetts.org/native-americans-revolutionary-war/.

"Bunker Hill." American Battlefield Trust, n.d. https://www.battlefields.org/learn/revolutionary-war/battles/bunker-hill.

Cathey, Kyla. "9 Women Who Helped Win the American Revolution." Mental Floss, March 30, 2021. https://www.mentalfloss.com/article/67905/9-women-who-helped-win-american-revolution.

Coleman, Colette. "7 Black Heroes of the American Revolution." History.com, February 12, 2020. https://www.history.com/news/black-heroes-american-revolution.

Collins, Elizabeth M. "Black Soldiers in the Revolutionary War." www.army.mil, n.d. https://www.army.mil/article/97705/black_soldiers_in_the_revolutionary_war.

"Comte De Grasse." American Battlefield Trust, n.d. https://www.battlefields.org/learn/biographies/comte-de-grasse.

"Crispus Attucks." American Battlefield Trust, n.d. https://www.battlefields.org/learn/biographies/crispus-attucks.

"Culper Spy Ring." George Washington's Mount Vernon, n.d. https://www.mountvernon.org/library/digitalhistory/digital-encyclopedia/article/culper-spy-ring/.

Cummings, Carol. "Our Italian Forefathers: Italian Contributions to American Independence." Sons of Italy Blog, June 16, 2015. https://osia.wordpress.com/2012/07/03/our-italian-forefathers-italian-contributions-to-american-independence/.

"The Declaration of Independence Charted a Path for All American Patriots." SoldierStrong, March 25, 2021. https://www.soldierstrong.org/mutually-pledge-lives-fortunes-sacred-honor/.

"Diary Sheds Light on Deborah Sampson, Who Fought in the Revolutionary War." Smithsonian.com. Smithsonian Institution, July 2, 2019. https://www.smithsonianmag.com/smart-news/diary-sheds-light-deborah-sampson-who-fought-revolutionary-war-180972547/.

"Education of Women during the Colonial Period Essay." Bartleby, n.d. https://www.bartleby.com/essay/Education-Of-Women-During-The-Colonial-Period-P3D5JKWYLCXW.

Evans, Farrell. "America's First Black Regiment Gained Their Freedom by Fighting against the British." History.com, February 3, 2021. https://www.history.com/news/first-black-regiment-american-revolution-first-rhode-island?cmpid=email-.

Ferling, John. "Myths of the American Revolution." Smithsonian.com. Smithsonian Institution, January 1, 2010. https://www.smithsonianmag.com/history/myths-of-the-american-revolution-10941835/.

"Friedrich Wilhelm Von Steuben." Wikipedia. Wikimedia Foundation, January 18, 2022. https://en.wikipedia.org/wiki/Friedrich_Wilhelm_von_Steuben.

"Great Bridge." American Battlefield Trust, n.d. https://www.battlefields.org/learn/revolutionary-war/battles/great-bridge.

Greenwalt, Phillip S. "British Perspective American Revolution." American Battlefield Trust, March 25, 2021. https://www.battlefields.org/learn/articles/british-perspective-american-revolution.

"History of Slavery in Massachusetts." Wikipedia. Wikimedia Foundation, December 7, 2021. https://en.wikipedia.org/wiki/History_of_slavery_in_Massachusetts.

Hylton, By: J. Gordon. "Before There Were 'Red' and 'Blue' States, There Were 'Free' States and 'Slave' States." Marquette University Law School Faculty Blog, October 28, 2021. https://law.marquette.edu/facultyblog/2012/12/before-there-were-red-and-blue-states-there-were-free-states-and-slave-states/.

"Jean-Baptiste Donatien De Vimeur, Comte De Rochambeau." Wikipedia. Wikimedia Foundation, January 3, 2022. https://en.wikipedia.org/wiki/Jean-Baptiste_Donatien_de_Vimeur,_comte_de_Rochambeau.

Klein, Christopher. "10 Things You May Not Know about Marquis De Lafayette." History.com, October 20, 2015. https://www.history.com/news/10-things-you-may-not-know-about-the-marquis-de-lafayette.

Klein, Christopher. "Why John Adams Defended British Soldiers in the Boston Massacre Trials." History.com, April 2, 2020. https://www.history.com/news/boston-massacre-trial-john-adams-dan-abrams.

Lewis, Jone Johnson. "Biography of Molly Pitcher, Heroine of the Battle of Monmouth." ThoughtCo, March 5, 2019. https://www.thoughtco.com/molly-pitcher-biography-3530670.

Lewis, Jone Johnson. "A Short History of Women's Property Rights in the U.S." ThoughtCo, July 13, 2019. https://www.thoughtco.com/property-rights-of-women-3529578.

"Lord Dunmore." American Battlefield Trust, n.d. https://www.battlefields.org/learn/biographies/lord-dunmore.

Makos, Isaac. "Roles of Native Americans during the Revolution." American Battlefield Trust, April 13, 2021. https://www.battlefields.org/learn/articles/roles-native-americans-during-revolution.

McBurney, Christian M. "Ann Bates: British Spy Extraordinaire." Journal of the American Revolution, August 28, 2016. https://allthingsliberty.com/2014/12/ann-bates-british-spy-extraordinaire/.

Michals, Debra, ed. "Deborah Sampson." National Women's History Museum, n.d. https://www.womenshistory.org/education-resources/biographies/deborah-sampson.

Michals, Debra, ed. "Nancy Hart." National Women's History Museum, n.d. https://www.womenshistory.org/education-resources/biographies/nancy-morgan-hart.

Michals, Debra, ed. "Sybil Ludington." National Women's History Museum, n.d. https://www.womenshistory.org/education-resources/biographies/sybil-ludington.

Mintz, Steven. "Historical Context: Facts about the Slave Trade and Slavery." Gilder Lehrman Institute of American History, n.d. https://www.gilderlehrman.org/history-resources/teaching-resource/historical-context-facts-about-slave-trade-and-slavery.

"Museum of the American Revolution." Museum of the American Revolution, n.d. https://www.amrevmuseum.org/.

National Geographic Society. "New England Colonies' Use of Slavery." National Geographic Society, December 10, 2019. https://www.nationalgeographic.org/article/new-england-colonies-use-slaves/5th-grade/.

"An Official Charter; a 'Lively Experiment.'" Brown University Timeline, n.d. https://www.brown.edu/about/history/timeline/official-charter-%E2%80%9Clively-experiment%E2%80%9D.

"Peter Salem." American Battlefield Trust, n.d. https://www.battlefields.org/learn/biographies/peter-salem.

"Prudence Wright." American Battlefield Trust, n.d. https://www.battlefields.org/learn/biographies/prudence-wright.

"Prudence Wright." Wikipedia. Wikimedia Foundation, October 17, 2021. https://en.wikipedia.org/wiki/Prudence_Wright.

"Revolutionary Spies." National Women's History Museum, November 9, 2017. https://www.womenshistory.org/articles/revolutionary-spies.

"Rhode Island's Royal Charter." State of Rhode Island, n.d. https://www.sos.ri.gov/divisions/civics-and-education/for-educators/themed-collections/rhode-island-charter.

Rindfleisch, Bryan. "The Stockbridge-Mohican Community, 1775-1783." Journal of the American Revolution, August 28, 2016. https://allthingsliberty.com/2016/02/the-stockbridge-mohican-community-1775-1783/.

"Salem Poor." Wikipedia. Wikimedia Foundation, January 2, 2022. https://en.wikipedia.org/wiki/Salem_Poor.

"Sarah Franklin Bache." Wikipedia. Wikimedia Foundation, November 30, 2021. https://en.wikipedia.org/wiki/Sarah_Franklin_Bache.

Schenawolf, Harry. "American Revolutionary War Cockades in Washington's Army." Revolutionary War Journal, July 8, 2019. https://www.revolutionarywarjournal.com/cockades/.

"Short History of the United States Flag." American Battlefield Trust, March 25, 2021. https://www.battlefields.org/learn/articles/short-history-united-states-flag.

"Slavery in New York." New York Historical Society. Accessed January 21, 2022. http://www.slaveryinnewyork.org/history.htm.

"Slavery in the United States." Wikipedia. Wikimedia Foundation, January 20, 2022. https://en.wikipedia.org/wiki/Slavery_in_the_United_States#Revolutionary_era.

Smith, Susan. "The Covered Bridge." Pepperell Historical Society, n.d. http://www.pepperellhistory.org/whispers/the-covered-bridge/.

Spencer-Wood, Suzanne M. "Creating a More Inclusive Boston Freedom Trail and Black Heritage Trail: An Intersectional Approach to Empowering Social Justice and Equality." International Journal of Historical Archaeology 25, no. 1 (2020): 207-71. https://doi.org/10.1007/s10761-020-00544-w.

"Spy Letters of the American Revolution." UM Clements Library, September 20, 2019. https://clements.umich.edu/exhibit/spy-letters-of-the-american-revolution/.

Stelloh, Tim. "Rhode Island Voters Drop 'Providence Plantations' from State Name." NBCUniversal News Group, November 5, 2020. https://www.nbcnews.com/politics/2020-election/rhode-island-voters-drop-providence-plantations-state-name-n1246501.

"Sybil Ludington: The 16-Year-Old Revolutionary Hero Who Rode Twice as Far as Paul Revere." www.amightygirl.com, n.d. https://www.amightygirl.com/blog?p=24115.

"Tadeusz Kościuszko." Wikipedia. Wikimedia Foundation, January 18, 2022. https://en.wikipedia.org/wiki/Tadeusz_Ko%C5%9Bciuszko.

Tierney, Kevin. "The Freedom Valley Chronicles: Hector Street and Edward 'Ned' Hector." MoreThanTheCurve, February 15, 2018. https://morethanthecurve.com/freedom-valley-chronicles-hector-street-edward-ned-hector/.

Tingley, Brett. "Get to Know the Brutal Artillery of the Revolutionary War." The Drive, December 1, 2019. https://www.thedrive.com/the-war-zone/28836/get-to-know-the-brutal-artillery-of-the-revolutionary-war.

"Trans-Atlantic Slave Trade - Database." Slave Voyages, n.d. https://www.slavevoyages.org/voyage/database.

Trenholm, Sandra. "Former Slave, Doctor Cuffee Saunders, 1781." The Gilder Lehrman Institute of american history, n.d. https://www.gilderlehrman.org/news/former-slave-doctor-cuffee-saunders-1781.

"Vermont 1777: Early Steps against Slavery." National Museum of African American History and Culture, February 15, 2018. https://nmaahc.si.edu/blog-post/vermont-1777-early-steps-against-slavery.

Wheatley, Phillis. "To His Excellency General Washington." Owl Eyes, n.d. https://www.owleyes.org/text/his-excellency.

"Women in the American Revolution: An Overlooked Force," n.d. https://sites.google.com/site/bryanthegirl/q1/writing/essays/women-in-the-revolution.

"Women Patriots in the American Revolution - Gale Blog ...," n.d. https://blog.gale.com/women-patriots-in-the-american-revolution/.

"Women's Rights Activity from 1776-1848." Women's Rights Activity from 1776-1848 | New York Heritage, n.d. https://nyheritage.org/exhibits/recognizing-womens-right-vote-new-york-state/womens-rights-activity-1776-1848.

Wood, Betty. "Slavery in Colonial Georgia - New Georgia Encyclopedia," n.d. https://www.georgiaencyclopedia.org/articles/history-archaeology/slavery-in-colonial-georgia/.

About the Author

Bestselling author, singer, songwriter, and musician Mifflin Lowe has had many books published, selling over 300,000 copies in five languages. His books include many children's books—*The True West* (Bushel & Peck); *Dad: The Man, The Myth, The Legend* (Bushel & Peck); *The Cuddle Book* (Familius); *Beasts by the Bunches* (Doubleday)—and three humor books for adults: *The Cheapskate's Handbook, I Hate Fun,* and *How To Be A Celebrity* (Price/Stern/Sloan). He has also performed his music for family audiences from New England to New Orleans, presenting works from his children's CDs *The King Who Forgot His Underpants, Wilton Wilberry and the Magical Christmas Wishing Well,* and *Beasts by the Bunches* (Caedmon/Harper & Row). Recently, his animated film script *The Awesome, Amazing, Occasionally Astonishing Adventures of Cowboy Howie* won the blue ribbon prize in the Sarasota Film Office TV/ME competition.

About the Illustrator

Wiliam is an illustrator and graphic designer. He graduated from Dong Nai College of Decorative Arts as one of the top students in his class. His work is included in many books, including *The True West* and *50 Real Heroes for Boys* (Bushel & Peck).

If you liked this book, please leave a review online at your favorite retailer. Honest reviews spread the word about Bushel & Peck—and help us make better books, too!

www.bushelandpeckbooks.com/pages/
nominate-a-school-or-organization

About Bushel & Peck Books

Bushel & Peck Books is a children's publishing house with a special mission. Through our Book-for-Book Promise™, we donate one book to kids in need for every book we sell. Our beautiful books are given to kids through schools, libraries, local neighborhoods, shelters, nonprofits, and also to many selfless organizations who are working hard to make a difference. So thank you for purchasing this book! Because of you, another book will find itself in the hands of a child who needs it most.

Why Literacy Matters

We can't solve every problem in the world, but we believe children's books can help. Illiteracy is linked to many of the world's greatest challenges, including crime, school dropout rates, and drug use. Yet impressively, just the presence of books in a home can be a leg up for struggling kids. According to one study, "Children growing up in homes with many books get three years more schooling than children from bookless homes, independent of their parents' education, occupation, and class. This is as great an advantage as having university educated rather than unschooled parents, and twice the advantage of having a professional rather than an unskilled father."[1]

Unfortunately, many children in need find themselves without adequate access to age-appropriate books. One study found that low-income neighborhoods have, in some US cities, only one book for every three hundred kids (compared to thirteen books for every one child in middle-income neighborhoods).[2]

With our Book-for-Book Promise™, Bushel & Peck Books is putting quality children's books into the hands of as many kids as possible. We hope these books bring an increased interest in reading and learning, and with that, a greater chance for future success.

1   M.D.R. Evans, Jonathan Kelley, Joanna Sikora & Donald J. Treiman. Family scholarly culture and educational success: Books and schooling in 27 nations. *Research in Social Stratification and Mobility.* Volume 28, Issue 2, 2010. 171-197.

2   Neuman, S.B. & D. Celano (2006). The knowledge gap: Effects of leveling the playing field for low- and middle-income children. *Reading Research Quarterly,* 176-201.

le, d'apres les meilleures & speciales Cartes angloises qui ont parues jusqu'ici par F.L. Güssefeld. Chez les Heritieres de Homann, l'an 17..

CANADA

PROVINCE QUEBEK

NEUSCHOTTLAND ACADIEN

St. Laurenz Flus

ATLANTISCHES MEER

Adirondaks oder Algonkins

Huron See

Ontario See

Michigan See

NH

M

M

C

NJ

PN

MRL

DW

VIRGINIEN

NORTH CAROLINA

SOUTH CAROLINA

GEORGIA

...IDA

In Staten Island.
1. Richmond.
In Neu Jersey.
2. Newark.
3. Elisabethtown.
4. Morristown.
In Pensylvanien.
5. Germantown.
6. Bristol.
7. Chester.
8. Millstown.
9. Ephrata.
10. Manheim.
11. Hummelstown.

CHARTE
über die XIII. vereinigte
Staaten von
NORD-AMERICA
Entworfen durch F. L. Güssefeld
und herausgegeben von den
Homännischen Erben
Mit Römisch Kayserl. Allergn.
Freyheit A.º 1784.

Erlæuterung der grosen Buchstaben.

M. Provinz Massachusets Bay. NH. New Hampshire.
R. Rhode-Island. C. Connecticut. NY. New York.
NJ. New Jersey. PNS Pensylvanien. DW. Delaware.
MRL. Maryland. Die übrigen vier Provinzen sind auf der Charte b...

Geographische Meilen 15. auf 1. Grad.

See-Meilen 20. auf einen Grad.

Englændis. Meilen 69 ½ auf einen Grad.

CONGRESS, JULY

he unanimous Declaration of the thirteen united States

When in the Course of human events, it becomes necessary for one people to dissolve the political bands

assume among the powers of the earth, the separate and equal station to which the Laws of Nat

should declare the causes which impel them to the separation. —————— We

with certain unalienable Rights, that among these are Life, Liberty and the pursuit of

powers fr   ment becom

Governmi   powers in such

will dicta   and transien

evils are   they are accu

wines a   is their duty,

been the   ich constrains

Britain   bject the estab

world   lesome and n

and pre   should be ob

POEMS

ON

VARIOUS SUBJECTS,